How other educators grade Carol Fuery

"Your approach motivates my students yet lets me stay in control." —Teacher, St. Petersburg, Florida

"Thinking back on my first year as a teacher, had someone provided such a valuable resource to me, I would have been a much more effective educator." —Superintendent, Sweeny, Texas

"Only someone who's been in the trenches with us could write Winning Year One, *a pertinent and inspirational book. I read it every August before I go back to school."* —Teacher, Houston, Texas

"Thanks to Are You Still Teaching?, *my 14th year was as exciting and rewarding for me—and for my seventh graders—as my first year of teaching."* —Teacher, St. Paul, Minnesota

Acknowledgments

Thanks to Cindy Pierce, a wonderful editor,
and
Jaye Boswell, an artist and teacher,
who created the illustrations.

Dedication

This book is dedicated with love to my three brothers—
ROBERT CARTEE BAILEY
WILLIAM F. BAILEY
JAMES CORBETT BAILEY

who were my original laugh mates and sailing companions. They, above all else, taught me the value of compromise.

Sanibel Sanddollar Publications, Inc.
Captiva Island, FL 33924

Copyright May 1990
Second Printing June 1991
Third Printing June 1993

Sanibel Sanddollar Publications
P. O. Box 461
Captiva Island, FL 33924
813 472-3459
ISBN 0-944295-03-7

Call Toll Free:
1-800-330-3459
FAX purchase order to: 813-472-0699
Discounts for large orders and for bookstores.

ARE
YOU
STILL
TEACHING?

A Survival Guide
To Keep You Sane

by
Carol Bailey Fuery

ILLUSTRATIONS
BY JAYE BOSWELL

A Letter
From A First Year Teacher—

Dear Ms. Fuery,

My first year of teaching has been filled with many trials and tribulations, many I caused. Students thought of me as a cold and uncaring person.

Many of the students liked the progress the bands were making but did not like the actual class. As a result, I lost several good students and more were on their way out.

The week before Thanksgiving, ten students decided to try to quit. I was given a meeting with both the principal and the superintendent. They took the time to explain that the kids liked what they were learning in class, but that they did not feel I "cared" about them as students.

I almost quit my job at that point. The principal explained that I appeared negative. I almost could not believe it! I knew that I was rarely positive, but . . . they informed me that I needed to make the students feel positive about band or I would not have a job next year.

Over Thanksgiving I went home to El Paso and visited my parents. It was at this time my mother showed me your book *Winning Year One, A Survival Guide for First Year Teachers.*

I found many of the things in your book sounded exactly like me. I read it from cover to cover, twice.

I am trying to change many of the aspects of my teaching that seem negative. I have even taken steps to be more caring and involved with the students. As a result the last two weeks have been much better. I now feel better about teaching. Class is better for the students and my personal sanity. I may even keep some of those who wanted to quit. In a nut shell, I can't thank you enough for your advice. . ."

Contents

Introduction
The Question This Book Will Answer

Appendix

ARE YOU
STILL TEACHING?

Introduction

Dear colleague,

This book was written for you, the experienced educator.

You are entering the over-burdened, underpaid, why-am-I-still teaching phase. As you gain experience, this profession should get easier. It doesn't.

In August/September, the letter arrives from your principal. "Welcome back to school." You ask yourself, Again? So soon?

You weigh the salary against the rewards and head back into the classroom for one last year. God help your family, your friends and your students because they struggle with you.

You sponsor clubs, earn advanced degrees, join professional groups and still you are searching.

You are on a familiar path. Teaching becomes a cycle, a rhythm, and a routine. Sometimes it becomes a deadly routine that isn't questioned.

The alarm rings. You eat breakfast hurriedly and rush to work numb.

1

You teach like a tape recorder, one that's been re-played too often.

You've even stopped asking yourself, Why am I teaching? What am I gaining? How am I growing?

Teach kids values, say the experts, yet the contradiction is that we don't value ourselves or our profession.

In our subconscious lies the nagging suspicion that we should be doing something that pays us better both financially and emotionally. We don't know what that elusive something is.

We spend our lives alternating between sulking and searching. Yet the choice is simple: Learn to enjoy teaching, or get out and do something else. I'm not advocating that you quit. I'm advocating that you stop playing victim, stop suffering and stop burdening others.

We can't change superintendents, schools boards, parents or principals. But we can change the one arena we control—the classroom.

Gaining power, achieving status, renewing ourselves and encouraging others—that's what this book is all about.

You are a survivor. Now, I'd like to help you keep your sanity.

The Question This Book Will Answer

Classes were changing. Hallways were packed with kids. It was the catch-your-breath time. My colleagues and I met briefly in the teachers' work area. Our cubbyhole gave us a brief respite.

In between sips of coffee, another teacher asked me about my writing. "When will you write a book for me?" she demanded.

At the time I was recuperating from surgery, and

about the last thing I wanted to do was start a new project. But . . .

Then my fellow teacher asked, "What do former students always ask us? 'Are you still teaching?' That would make a good title." She was right.

We like our memories of the past left unchanged. We want our favorite teachers still teaching. It's acceptable if they retire or die, we just don't want them selling used cars.

Ideally we want them in the same classroom, the same school and the same life. It gives us security. It makes sense that good teachers stay.

Yet we are all aware of the teacher who retires and never leaves the building. Kids suffer.

The difference between a non-effective teacher and an effective one is simple. The non-effective teacher does half of what's expected and complains bitterly. The good teacher does twice what's expected and feels guilty that it's not enough.

Are You Still Teaching? means are you still growing, supporting and helping kids? Most importantly, are you still creating an exciting life for yourself?

That is the question this book will answer. That is my gift to you.

Carol Fuery
Sanibel Island, Florida

1 *Are You A Career Teacher?*

I didn't realize I was a career teacher until I quit. Actually, I didn't quit. I took a leave of absence, but emotionally the experience was the same.

I did fine over the summer. Problems for me began in August. I'd wake up every morning at three and stay awake until dawn. After a week of insomnia, I went to a friend who was a doctor.

He explained that because I'd taught for eighteen years and had taken the year's leave, I was mourning the loss of my job. I laughed but realized that he was right. As soon as I admitted that I did miss school, I was able to get a good night's rest.

I had a difficult time facing my ambivalence. I loved my new found freedom, yet missed the kids. Most of us who have taught longer than six years are career teachers. And we either don't know it or won't admit it.

As one friend of mine started her nineteenth year, she expressed her ambivalence this way: "Every year the

4

kids get better and better." Then she added. "I love teaching but I don't plan to do this forever."

That's the heart of the problem. We don't want to admit to being a career teacher because we don't want to feel stuck. We dream that we'll find another job that will pay us better, give us less responsibility as well as more day-to-day satisfaction.

Maybe what we need to do is start appreciating what's good about our career. Let's examine some misconceptions that might be clouding our thinking.

Fact/Fallacy #1: Teachers Have Limited Power

The number one power position in the school is the teacher. Why? Because no one else has the influence that we do on the lives of the kids. Principals and administrators are busy with meetings and reports; they don't work in the front-line position.

I consider myself a small business owner. I rent office space, my classroom, from the principal. Sure, I have a curriculum guide to follow, but I'm still an independent operator. When my classroom door closes, I have lots of freedom. As the teacher I'm the CEO, the chief executive officer.

Fact/Fallacy #2: Teaching Lacks Advancement

Nothing could be farther from the truth. The reason we believe this statement is because we've heard it many times. We have never learned to value the skills that make us good educators. I've known teachers who left the field to go into banking, law, home building, landscaping, writing, etc. The possible careers beyond the classroom are limited only by our imaginations.

Why are teachers successful in other careers? Because the same public relations, motivating and communicating skills gained through working with kids can be applied to other fields.

The ability to win over thirty reluctant learners can help you motivate a business staff.

Start today to appreciate your people skills. Realize they are transferable.

Fact/Fallacy #3: Teaching Is Routine

It can be. But so are marriages. And some marriages simply die of boredom. Whether it's work or love, new ideas create interest. And who's responsible? We are.

Vary the tune. Teach something new. Surprise the class.

Every spring when routines really get deadly, a friend of mine ignites enthusiasm with a unique idea. She teaches third grade and takes a week's "vacation." She sends in her identical cousin from France. Then, she fakes a French accent, borrows her neighbor's clothes and teaches a unit on France. The "French teacher" is well loved.

Any change in routine is exciting and will spark interest for both kids and teachers. It also increases learning.

A study was made in the 1930's that showed changes in the environment improved the productivity of a General Electric plant. And the changes were small. When lights were dimmed, productivity increased. When hours were varied, productivity increased. Do something to vary your routine, and watch the kids learn.

Fact/Fallacy # 4: Teachers Are Underpaid

I feel that the intrinsic rewards of teaching far outweigh my paycheck. I am constantly running into former students. They greet me with enthusiasm and have fond memories of our time together.

I don't know what "price" I can put on holding a former student's baby.

Sure my paycheck doesn't go as far as I'd like. Yet almost all of my friends in other professions aren't thrilled with their salaries either. We do have a choice. We can supplement our income. A wonderful friend of mine who's a great teacher also works part time at Sears. With a family and school, she's a busy lady but very happy.

My cousin used to teach Shakespeare, now she slings burgers for big bucks. She's a MacDonald's manager. She enjoys the money and working with young people. And she still talks about returning to the classroom one day.

Now that we've examined a few facts and fallacies about teaching, let's answer that most important question.

WHY DO I TEACH?

I teach because . . .

I teach because I like working with kids. I have a real estate license, but I'd rather sell poetry than property. I'd rather read Hamlet than real estate ads. Also, I like having my hands on someone else's future.

Robert Hahler, a columnist for the Concord Monitor, wrote Christa McAuliffe's biography. He said, "I felt an obligation to tell her story for history's sake. I wanted her to be remembered 50 years from now not as an astronaut, but as a teacher . . . which is what she was and how she wanted to be remembered."

Christa called going into space the "ultimate field trip." When she was one of the 20 finalists and was asked, "Why do you want to go?" she answered quickly, "I believe I can be a symbol for all American teachers."

She has achieved immortality because she lives on

in the hearts of her students and in the hearts of teachers everywhere.

Christa McAuliffe said it best, "I touch the future, I teach." Christa knew who she was and what she wanted. She affected our lives because she found happiness as a teacher.

BENEFITS OF TEACHING

1. Guaranteed salary

As teachers, we may not be paid as much as we'd like, but our salary is dependable. Most school districts don't declare bankruptcy.

And when we compare our salary to other careers, we work a ten-month year.

2. Vacations

I couldn't teach if I didn't have my summers free. Those two weeks in December and another week in the spring really help to keep me sane. Friends of mine who work for the Postal Service don't even like the month of December. Can you blame them?

3. Seniority

If you've taught ten years in ten different schools, you can't take advantage of this benefit. If you're happy where you are, stay put and build your reputation.

I enjoy teaching seniors, but in two years I might need a change. Having seniority gives me the chance to choose.

THE QUESTION WE'RE TOO BUSY TO ASK

Writing down goals makes our dreams real. Deciding what we really want is one of life's toughest decisions. Four years ago, I had a conversation about goals with my friend. It changed my life.

We were discussing what we wanted to do "when we grew up." I said that I'd like to write a book for new teachers. My friend, Ron, grabbed a pencil and started writing. "Give me the chapter titles."

The next morning I had a long list of good ideas. I decided to organize my thoughts in a short letter. I mailed the ideas for the book to educational publishers, pretending that the book was already written.

I received some encouraging rejection notes. Then I got a call from the president of a major publishing company. He asked, "Is the book written?" I told him it was. Then he said, "Send me the first five chapters."

I hung up the phone and started writing. For the next three months, life was hectic. I completed the manuscript over the summer, and in the fall, the publisher rejected it completely. He told me he didn't know how to promote it.

I was devastated. I felt like a failure. Then I formed my own company and published my first book, *Winning Year One,* myself. Now, seven years and almost 50,000 copies later, I realize his rejection was the best thing that could have happened to me.

I learned a valuable lesson. If we concentrate on what we really want, we'll succeed no matter what challenges get in our way. More than working hard, we need to focus on what's important to us.

KNOWING WHAT YOU WANT

Write goals for yourself only. Make them as specific as possible. If under the heading "Personal goals" you write, "Go skiing," be sure to set a date. That creates a deadline. Spend some time answering the next few questions.

> *If I had six months to live and all the money I needed, how would I spend my time?*
>
> *If I were to die tomorrow, what three things would my husband/wife/lover and/or family miss the most?*
>
> *What things would I miss the most?*
>
> *What accomplishments in my teaching career am I most proud of?*
>
> *In the next five months, what three major goals do I hope to accomplish with my teaching?*
>
> *What five major personal goals have I set for myself? Put a deadline for accomplishing each one.*

Keep a list of four or five current goals in a place you'll see everyday. I keep mine on my bulletin board above my desk. The goals we write are road maps, and like all travel plans, they need frequent updating.

When I began this chapter, I asked if you were a career teacher. You will know that answer at the end of this book. In the next chapter, we will look at another facet of our career: the way we use our time.

SUMMARY:

1. Are you a career teacher?
2. We can be successful elsewhere.
3. Teaching creates intrinsic rewards.
4. Career teachers enjoy seniority.
5. Set specific goals with deadlines.

2 If It's Only Tuesday, Why Am I So Frazzled?

Someone once said about work that we should be good at it, we should feel successful in it and we shouldn't do too much of it. The most unhappy teachers I know are those who do too much of it.

I don't mind if colleagues are working harder than they need to, I just wish they would not tell me about it. I wish they would keep their efforts a secret. Why?

Because we all feel guilty. Regardless of how much we accomplish in the classroom, it is never enough. Let's stop. Congratulate ourselves on what we can accomplish, which is considerable, and let the rest go.

11

The "CARRY EXCESS PAPERS HOME" SYNDROME

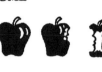

At the end of the day, you have seen teachers in the parking lot loading up their car trunks. They almost need a shopping cart.

I have a problem with carrying excessive amounts of papers home. Many nights they won't make it from the car to the dining room table. They take the ride home and the ride back, left untouched in the trunk. They are painful reminders of work left unfinished.

Procrastination comes in many forms, and it does one thing well. It lowers our self-esteem. After a day of teaching, that's the last thing I need.

WE ARE NEVER FINISHED

The problem with our profession is that we're never finished. When I was in college, I worked the breakfast shift as a waitress. When quitting time came, I walked out the door with cash and no responsibility. Until the alarm clock rang the next morning, I didn't think of work again.

With teaching, when do we think we'll be through? Not when we retire. A friend, now retired, lives on an island near me. She was a teacher, a librarian and a principal. She spends her time now bird watching and beach walking.

I see her frequently. On one of my visits she told me that she still dreams about the kids. When I asked her why, she answered, "Because the problems they had were never solved."

We'll be finished with teaching when we die. No sooner. Face this reality, and stop feeling guilty. Stop trying to be Super Teacher. Let's do the best we possibly can and accept our limitations.

If carrying excessive papers home every night is counter-productive, then we need to get more done at school. Here are some ways that may help.

1. Write An End-of-Day List

Everyone talks about the "to do" list. That's important, but so is the list you write at the end of the day.

When the final bell rings, clear your desk. Sound impossible? Stack those papers in drawers or on the floor underneath the desk.

Now write a brief list of four to five items you must do the next day. Number the items in the order of their importance. This sheet of paper becomes your blueprint for the next day's work. When you return in the morning, it's easy to focus on your plan.

2. Arrive At School Early

Arriving thirty-five minutes early will make a big difference in your day. Head for the classroom and pick up your list. If the first item says, "Grade papers," gather up the papers and go into hiding.

Find a quiet corner in the library and give yourself thirty minutes of concentrated grading time. Because there are no interruptions, you will be able to work quickly.

Don't be a perfectionist. That's neurotic. Mark one or two specific skills (the ones you've just taught) and let the rest of the mistakes go.

Papers held three days or more lose their impact. Kids forget. They learn more when papers are returned the next day.

Your thirty minutes of concentrated effort will become a valuable asset to your day. And it's one way of keeping papers out of the car trunk.

3. Share Everything

If I'm teaching Macbeth, why should I write the tests? I get help from the teacher who is a Shakespeare fanatic. She has been teaching for many years, and she has a file drawer on Macbeth.

You and I all know the teacher who hoards materials and won't share. It's a terrible waste of time. Realizing that other teachers can be our allies is a big step in our own development. Find willing colleagues and give and get the material that you need.

4. Just Say No

The most powerful word in the English language is "no." Why do we feel guilty or obligated to say yes when we want to say no?

Perhaps we are afraid of hurting someone else's feelings. But what about our feelings and our sanity? I sometimes say yes to a request because I want to please. Many times I don't give the request the thought it deserves.

It is much better to say, "Let me think about it. I'll check my calendar and let you know."

Take time to think, then learn to say no and protect your limited time.

14

5. Employ Your Secretary

You have a secretary. She is the school's secretary as well, but she also works for you. She is a valuable person, and we are all aware of her influence.

She can take all your school phone calls and give you the messages. Keep a list of the names and numbers and return them all at one time.

Taking a phone call at school wastes valuable time. It interrupts your day. Usually the call will come from a parent, and the worst thing we can do is talk with parents when we are unprepared.

When you make the phone call, then you are the one in charge. I return all my phone calls at six p.m. That's when I can usually catch parents at home.

6. Learn to Hide

Work areas in schools are not conducive to work . In order to get things done, we must create our own space. The cafeteria in early morning or late afternoon is a good bet. The library is, too. Just find a quiet corner away from colleagues.

7. Complete Tasks at Unusual Times

Friday afternoons are good times to get things done. Why? Because I have the building to myself. The only cars in the parking lot belong to the custodians and one administrator.

Most of us make the mistake of using the copy machine on Monday mornings, usually five minutes before class starts. There's a line. First the paper supply runs out, then the toner. You get five copies and the machine quits. Frustration and it's not even first hour.

Better to spend a little time on a Friday afternoon running off materials.

I gave this suggestion to a group in Colorado. After my seminar, the school's principal told me that he hoped his teachers wouldn't follow my advice. He explained that Friday afternoons were the only time he could get caught up on his work.

8. Use Computers/Word Processors

A. For Correspondence

Unfortunately, the school secretary won't answer your mail. But your word processor can. Keep stock or form letters in memory. These include letters to parents. I have included my letters in the back of this book. You may use them or borrow some ideas and write your own.

B. For Grades

Kids need to know how they are doing. Give grades once a week or every other week and watch it work as a motivator. Your students will have a chance to complete assignments before it's too late.

Computers make grade-keeping easy. Once you start using them you will never go back to the old-fashioned methods.

C. For Storage

Why fill up file drawers? You can put information on a disk and it can be easily retrieved. You may want to invest in a compatible home word processor.

A Word About Computers

There are many helpful uses for computers and word processors in the classroom. Yet many of us hesitate to learn the few skills necessary to make our lives easier.

A friend of mine is in a new school. Her department has a room full of computers for the kids to use. She regularly takes half of her English classes down to the computer room to type their essays.

The kids love writing and find editing easy.

Want to place bets on how many other teachers use this computer room? None. That is right. None.

My friend has offered to teach the other teachers, but so far no one has taken her up on the offer.

It really is too bad that in this particular situation, teachers are preventing their students from enjoying the equipment that is available.

Learn to use the computers and word processors in your school to save your valuable time.

CREATING SLICES OF TIME

I live on Sanibel Island in Florida where interval ownership is popular. Visitors purchase condominiums for one or more weeks of the year. One company uses a popular advertising slogan to describe interval ownership. Their weeks are called, "vacations by the slice."

That is true about our lives. Most of us get a short time for work or for play. We can't wait until we have unlimited hours for important projects. Instead we create small slices of time.

I have some suggestions for making better use of those moments.

1. Commute Time

I have a forty-five minute drive to school. Listening to motivational tapes, music or my own thoughts helps me arrive refreshed. But the best part of that drive is when I tune in a two-minute inspirational message given by a local minister. When he is through, I turn down the radio and concentrate on the message. It gives me a lift.

How do you use your commute time? If you share the drive with a colleague, do you try to say positive things to one another?

Notice something beautiful on your drive to school. Listen to an inspirational tape and use the commuting time well.

2. Lunch Time

The average school cafeteria is as pleasant and peaceful as an insane asylum. Cafeterias are over-crowded and the noise level is deafening.

Carry in a healthy lunch. Find a quiet place and enjoy the peace.

3. Alone Time

Being alone, even for five minutes may be impossible, but it is necessary for our mental health. After lunch, I slip quietly back into my classroom and lock the door behind me.

I pull together two chairs, stretch out and close my eyes. I don't fall asleep or chant. I do take five minutes to clear my mind of all problems. I pretend that I'm looking at black velvet.

After this short interval, it is amazing how good I feel. By the end of the day, I am more relaxed. When I am too busy to take this time, I really feel it by sixth hour.

We make appointments and commitments all day

long. Maybe it is time that we decided to make an appointment with ourselves. When is your alone time?

4. Exercise Time

I dislike exercise. The gear, the drive and the sweat. But I love the people in my aerobics class. I enjoy the instructor and the music. But what I like best is when class ends and I get a rush of energy.

I am forty-three years old. Time is no longer on my side. Getting in shape and staying in shape may be tough, but the alternatives are worse.

Teaching takes its toll in stress. I have had friends in their forties and fifties suffer heart attacks and strokes. Regular exercise keeps me fit and helps me cope with the daily stresses.

And if your exercise program isn't fun, you won't stick with it. Find something you enjoy doing.

5. Social Time

Several years ago, I became involved with a community group of actors and actresses. We all hold full-time jobs and manage to produce three to five shows a year. The group's members change for each play, so there are always new people to meet.

During rehearsals, we grow close. We become almost a family. The fact that no one else in the theatre group teaches school is refreshing to me. When we're together, we have production problems to discuss.

Just like any other profession, we need time away from our colleagues. Find a social group away from educators, and it will do wonders for your perspective and your morale.

THE BALANCING ACT

In this chapter I hope that you've gained a few ideas for helping you feel less frantic. Living well means managing time well. Sometimes to keep our sanity, we need to slow down our lives.

A fast-track experience affects us all, even former President Reagan. In his farewell address to the nation, he said that he often was "going too fast in a car someone else was driving."

Gaining control of our lives means gaining control of our time. When we have energy and enthusiasm, we can get more done. That's why the next chapter deals with putting ourselves behind the wheel of our own motivation.

SUMMARY:

1. Leave an "end of day" list.
2. Arrive early. Hide.
3. Share all materials.
4. Use your secretary and word processor.
5. Create slices of time: commute, lunch, alone, exercise and social.

3 *Does My Motivation Need a Jump Start?*

A young gas station attendant was working in a rural Florida town. The first car of the day came roaring in and the couple sitting in the front seat looked like they hadn't spoken to each other for the last two hundred miles.

Eager to please, the attendant rushed over to wash the windshield. The woman who was driving rolled down her window. She shouted, "Don't wash my side. Wash his. All the driving's done over there."

When it applies to motivation, we're in the driver's seat. We can have supportive colleagues, concerned parents and helpful administrators. But if we walk into the classroom feeling depressed and defeated, all our attempts at motivating kids will fail.

Maybe our batteries aren't dead yet. They just need a jump start.

This chapter is designed to give you the spark to re-start your energy and enthusiasm. First we'll look at one of the major causes for low energy—boredom.

WHY IS BOREDOM USEFUL?

If we need something to make us feel enthusiastic and motivated, perhaps it is because we are bored.

Boredom is defined as a state of dissatisfaction. When we are bored, we have a passive attitude toward life. We hope the external world will supply some satisfaction.

How do we get relief? We need to become the source of our own pleasure. Action is our best defense. We need to find joy in what we do. Boredom is like anxiety in that it alerts us that all is not well. We need to do something to improve our lives.

How Do We Improve Our Lives?

The husband asks his wife what she wants for her twentieth wedding anniversary. The wife answers, "I'd like a divorce." Husband says, "I hadn't planned to spend that much."

When it applies to renewing our energies, how much are we willing to spend in terms of time and commitment? Perhaps what we need is more variety.

WAYS TO CREATE ENERGY

1. Find a Cause and Make It Yours

Eugene Lang gave a speech in 1981 to the graduating class of P.S. 121 elementary school in Harlem. He committed himself to providing a college education to all sixty-one members of the sixth grade class. The one stipulation was that they had to graduate from high school.

22

He caught the media's attention and gained scholarship programs from people like New York's Governor, Mario Cuomo. He also caught the children's attention.

Of the original class, fifty-two still visit him. Almost all have completed high school and thirty-six are attending college.

Eugene Lang doesn't think his ideas are creative. "What we have done is show these kids we care. Each individual relationship makes it worthwhile."

He didn't just fund their educations, but he also encouraged the kids along the way. "I found that the promise of a scholarship has a placebo effect. My promise would have meant very little if we hadn't been there throughout the following years, aware of what was happening in the students' lives, continually renewing their sense of motivation, their sense of coping."

There was no straight line to the students' graduation. Progress was erratic with students veering off the track. "I offered persistence, hope and confidence."

Eugene Lang was willing to pay the price of time and commitment. He established the "I Have A Dream Foundation" to insure the students' education.

"This is more important to me than anything else I've ever done in my life. The one thing I take credit for is that I knew a good thing when I saw it."

Extra-Curricular/Extra Celestial

In order to be effective in re-vitalizing our energies, we don't have to do anything as grand as Eugene Lang. Even small contributions can work miracles with kids.

Over the years I have been involved in various extracurricular school functions which have helped to keep me motivated. They have included teaching modeling, organizing a literary magazine, managing a self-study of our school and forming a professional group of

English teachers.

My pay was three cents an hour and all the ego I could stand. But I considered the work as energizing as a good college course. Did the activities help me keep my enthusiasm for teaching? Yes.

Could the projects have eventually burned me out? Perhaps. That is why switching activities and doing a variety of things you enjoy is the key.

2. Break Down the Walls

The moment that you come up with a good idea that will help kids, you will get the negative remarks. Consider them a compliment—you are threatening the status quo and mediocrity. The more negative comments, the better your idea.

Here are some statements that stop creativity and change:

1. *It's not in the curriculum.*
2. *You can't teach that.*
3. *It is against school policy.*
4. *It will never work.*
5. *They'll never let you do that.*
6. *It will cost too much.*
7. *There is no money in the budget for that.*
8. *We did that last year. It didn't work.*

Never allow similar remarks to keep you from achieving your dreams with kids.

3. Find A New Teacher

Becoming a mentor for a new teacher will do much more than you can ever imagine. While you share your expertise, a new teacher shares her energy.

I've spent over eighteen years getting help and developing myself as a teacher. It's about time I gave something back. And that's the point. To repay the people who gave me a push or a pat on the back, I help train a new teacher. And that new teacher trains and rejuvenates me.

The late Eric Hoffer said, "Those who invest themselves in becoming all they can become and those who invest themselves in helping others become all they can become, are involved in the most important work on the face of the earth; they are helping to complete God's plan."

Become a mentor and discover the rewards.

4. Positive Self-Talk

During my forty-five minute commute to school, I play a mental tape that is my self-talk. Here are some of the phrases that help give me a lift.

This is going to be a great day.
God made this morning and it is beautiful.
I'm lucky to be teaching. I'm lucky to be alive.
I have the power to make this the best day ever.
I know that something good will happen to
  me today.
I have strength and endurance.
I am in total control. I will win.
All the world and its opportunities are before me.

Negative thinking becomes a destructive habit that we don't need. Try re-phrasing negative thoughts.

One high school principal in Fort Lauderdale did just that. He tried a week long experiment with his faculty.

Staff, administrators, and teachers tried saying only positive statements to one another. At the end of the week, one teacher remarked, "When we couldn't say anything negative, I was surprised at how little we had to talk about."

Kids deserve to see our best side. With positive talk, we can help create the motivation that we need.

5. Subscribe To Professional Journals, Join Professional Organizations and Get Involved

One of our best investments is to subscribe to professional journals. They give new ideas and help us improve our skills. Subscriptions to magazines can get expensive. Try sharing a subscription or persuading your department chair or school librarian to invest in the magazine. Then all teachers will benefit.

All of us can improve and sharpen our skills. Conferences and conventions give us a chance to meet teachers from other areas who have the same problems and concerns.

I remember a conversation I had with a colleague about attending a state conference. He felt that by reading his professional journals, he'd learn everything he needed to know about new trends in teaching.

He was right to a point. However, one of the main reasons I attend conferences is to interact with the speakers and other teachers. I gain much in the informal activities. The fifteen-minute coffee break between sessions or the cocktail hour at sunset are valuable for meeting people and sharing ideas.

6. Anticipate the Seasons and Slumps

Some times of the year are easier to teach than others. Kids are fairly motivated in August and September. The first slump occurs in October.

Many state conventions are held in October, and I'm convinced it's to help us get through this first hurdle.

November and December move quickly because we have so many vacations. But watch out for January.

Teaching in January is similar to standing at the top of a mountain and being told by the ski instructor that, yes, you will be able to ski all the way down to the bottom. What's the prize at the bottom? Spring break.

In January, try to teach something that will help your own motivation. Look over the curriculum and do something unusual and fun. It will do wonders for your own and your students' energy.

After spring break is the second toughest time to teach. You've already guessed the worst time. It's June. The longer we teach in June, the less excited we become. When we have to spend the greater part of June making up snow days, teaching is drudgery.

May and June are rough because we are tired. Also our patience is at a low ebb. What can we do about it? One friend of mine teaches seventh grade science. She saves her sex education unit for May. She also tells her students that if they aren't mature enough to handle this subject, then they can attend another class. Her kids are well behaved and eager to learn.

How do I cope with May and June? I go shopping. I have a bumper sticker on my car that says, "When the going gets tough, the tough go shopping."

Find a way to cope with May and June. Teaching something fun, planning carefully, and giving yourself small rewards will help you get through the seasons and slumps.

7. *Take An Active Role In Rebuilding Enthusiasm*

All the skills and knowledge in the world won't help us be the best teachers unless we are enthusiastic.

Our enthusiasm is the engine that runs our lives.

Someone once said that "Nothing great is ever accomplished without enthusiasm." Enthusiastic people have energy. They get that energy not by doing more work, but by taking a constructive break from the daily routine.

What ways do you use to refresh yourself? I walk thirty minutes in the afternoons. I also take an aerobics class three times a week. After a little exercise, it is amazing how trivial problems seem.

What methods do you use to replenish your energies? What pleasure are you putting into your life?

When we go into the classroom feeling motivated, our kids will too. Their motivation is what we'll discuss next.

SUMMARY:

1. Find a cause.
2. Become a mentor.
3. Use positive self-talk.
4. Read journals and join professional organizations.
5. Refresh your energy with exercise.

4 *Motivating The Ungrateful Dead*

The art teacher was walking around the third grade classroom, helping individuals with their drawings. She stopped at one girl's desk. "Sally, what's that?"

Without hesitation, the young girl responded, "It's a picture of God."

"Well, we don't know what God looks like."

"You will when I get done."

We need that kind of blind confidence to motivate kids in a classroom. We can't force our students to cooperate or to succeed. There is, however, a great deal we can do to set up an atmosphere in the classroom where kids want to achieve.

Motivation involves creating an incentive. The three factors of motivation are reward, recognition and responsibility.

WHY THE VALUE OF REWARD IS UNIMPORTANT

We all remember B. F. Skinner's admonition, "Those actions which are rewarded are repeated." What we have heard less often is that the value of reward is not as important as the recognition from others. And that is priceless.

The trouble with some reward systems is that they are designed to discourage the teacher. If a reward system takes a great deal of record-keeping, I won't be motivated to even give it a try.

Some veteran teachers say that kids will succeed without rewards. They are partly right. Some kids will succeed no matter what. But most kids need that extra push that the reward provides.

WHY REPORT CARDS DON'T MOTIVATE

Report cards aren't always the power tool we'd like to imagine. For one thing, grades are given to kids too infrequently for them to be effective. Every nine weeks or once every six weeks doesn't provide enough urgency. Kids think about report cards the day before they come out, and the day or two after they've been distributed. That's it.

The Best Kept Secret

Grades can be motivating if kids are given frequent chances to find out how they are doing, then given an opportunity to make up missed work. An ideal situation is to let kids average their grades once a week. That puts the urgency back into using grades.

Letters Home

Report cards in themselves don't motivate kids, but

letters sent home, do.

I suggest beginning the year with a letter of introduction. A letter of congratulations follows. This second letter needs to be sent no later than the fourth week of the school year.

A third letter follows in late fall, a fourth in the spring and a fifth at the end of the year.

How Does The Student Earn Complimentary Letters?

They need to have all their work turned in with an average of a C or better. I have included sample letters at the end of the book. You may use them or write your own.

If you take the power of the letter seriously, your kids will too. Your attitude toward the reward and its power is most important for its success.

Letter Presentation

Make the presentation of letters an Oscar Awards Night affair. Your students are going to read these letters, so hand them an envelope. After they finish reading, they can fold and place the letter in the envelope.

What about students who don't earn a complimentary letter? You have an option. I have enclosed at the end of the book the letter that says, "Let's work on this problem together." The other students in the class don't need to know that this is not a congratulatory letter.

If you choose not to use the optional second letter, you might discover how powerful the letters really become. Students will be asking what they need to do to earn a letter. Make-up work should have a short deadline, not over two days.

I used to wonder why my high school students

were motivated by a form letter in ditto blue ink. Then I realized that the recognition from the entire class was the incentive.

CLASS HONOR ROLL

Grades don't necessarily motivate kids, but peer pressure works beautifully. Mid-way through the grading period, post a class honor roll.

Getting one's name on the class honor roll has the same requirements as a congratulatory letter. All work must be turned in and the student needs a C average or better. A piece of construction paper and five minutes to list students' first names is all that's needed.

How Effective Are Class Honor Rolls?

I have had parents tell me, "This is the first time Steve's name has ever been on the honor roll." I have also watched in amazement as some of the toughest kids in a low-level senior English class dropped by the classroom at lunchtime to show their buddies that their name was on the list.

A wall in the classroom is saved for the honor roll display. One colleague calls it the Wall of Fame. I've sometimes encouraged a little friendly competition by telling each class that if their group has the most names on the class list, they'll earn a special privilege or party.

Handing out letters and listing names on honor rolls gives kids the status they crave and rewards their efforts.

RECOGNITION

Everyone craves recognition. It's one of those needs that follows us from cradle to grave. Even people in old folks homes will vie for a visitor's attention.

Yet there comes a time in our growing up where it

is no longer acceptable to ask for recognition. The five-year-old can yell to big brother, "Hey watch me do a cartwheel." And hopefully the older sibling will say, "Great job. Do it again. You're terrific."

A teenager still needs the recognition but has outgrown the privilege of requesting it.

A friend of mine attended a seminar on self-esteem. The speaker asked the group to think of a time when they had accomplished something and had not received the praise they deserved. The leader further explained that anytime during his lecture, they could raise their hand, tell what it was they had accomplished, and receive a standing ovation. Twice the speaker was interrupted by applause.

Why? Because of the need for recognition.

HOW DO WE GIVE KIDS STANDING OVATIONS?

1. Share All Successes With The Class

Let kids know you're interested in their successes both inside and outside of school. Share announcements about awards and achievements. Clip newspaper articles that mention the school or individual students.

2. Share Good Papers With The Class

Sharing papers, innovative ideas or outstanding test answers is one way to compliment a student in front of the group. I find that some of the most creative answers don't come from my "A" students, but usually from my "D" or "C" students who rarely get a chance at recognition.

3. Use Students' Names

Remembering a person's name is a compliment.

Use the student's name when greeting or asking for responses to questions. Some states now require, as part of teachers' evaluations, the use of students' names during question/answer periods. If you fail to use the student's name you lose points on the evaluation.

4. Remember Personal Facts

Asking about an older brother or a sports activity can do wonders to build personal relationships. During the first week of class, have students write autobiographies.

Using information from this paper, I write phrases next to the student's name in the grade book. I might write, "five brothers" or "soccer." Then when there's a few minutes before or after class, I use that information to ask personal questions.

The reaction I get is one of pleasant surprise. How did you know I play soccer? It's a compliment that we care about our kids enough to take a few minutes to relate to them.

5. Apologize, Especially When It's Not Your Fault

Airline companies understand the power of an apology. When a flight is delayed or turbulence keeps the stewardess from serving beverages, a soft voice will announce: "I'm sorry, but we will be unable to serve drinks this afternoon."

It's not the stewardess' fault that we're going through inclement weather, but the apology smoothes over the inconvenience.

There are days when we get constant interruptions from the office, or the air-conditioner breaks during a heat wave. An apology softens the difficulty.

Saying something like: "I am sorry that the air isn't

working. I know it's warm, but I really do appreciate your cooperation. You're working diligently in spite of the conditions," acts as a motivator.

RESPONSIBILITY

By expecting success, we hold kids responsible for it. An expectation is a compliment that says, "I value you. I trust you to succeed." The minute we lower our expectations, we send an invitation to fail.

Chuck and Sally of the Peanuts cartoon fame were having a conversation. Sally was upset and remarked, "The teacher failed me, Chuck! That means I'm a dumb person. . . I know a lot of people who aren't as smart as they think they are . . . I just don't want to be as dumb as I think I am."

As Sally's teacher, we need to give her some chance at success. We need to expect the best from her. Expectations shape lives.

Remember the Harvard experiment by psychologist Robert Rosenthal in the mid-sixties? Teachers were told to watch for children who would show high academic achievement. Although the children's names were marked at random, scores for these students who were expected to excel showed dramatic improvement.

Follow-up studies focused on the reasons. The teachers were more demanding. They gave the "brighter" kids harder work. They expected right answers.

A 1981 *Psychology Today* article on the gifted explained the results this way: "When teachers are told students have high potential, whether the students turn out to be gifted or not, the teachers look, smile and nod at them more often. They also teach them more content, set higher goals for them, call on them more often and give them more time to answer."

It is no wonder that the favored kids do so well.

Beware of False Assumptions

When we expect less from kids, we demand less. And a poor performance is what we get. Kids can change remarkably within a nine-week period, and yet sometimes we still see the student as a "weak learner." Even when the student does well, we are sometimes reluctant to accept his progress. We become trapped in our false assumptions.

The Fix It Model

We are told that students have certain defects and that it is our job to fix what is wrong. I think we would have a much better chance if we worked from a strength model.

Perhaps our teaching would be more effective if we were told that kids have certain abilities. It is our job to begin where kids are strong, build on their successes and use them to turn areas of weakness around.

Expecting Success

We do kids a disservice by not expecting much from them. Harold Kushener in his book, *When All You've Ever Wanted Isn't Enough*, describes it best.

"We misunderstand human nature when we think we're helping people by not expecting very much from them. To be human is no excuse for laziness. God pays us a compliment by demanding more from us than from any other living creature. It may be difficult to work hard and be good, but it's a lot more difficult to be told you don't have what it takes to be smart or to be good so you're excused from trying."

Expectation, accountability and responsibility all work together in helping us bring out the best in our kids.

Next we will discuss how to bring out a student's success by using the classroom environment.

SUMMARY:

1. Remember the value of recognition.
2. Report cards don't motivate kids.
3. Reward through letters/honor rolls.
4. Share successes. Use students' names.
5. Remember personal tidbits.
6. Apologize, especially when it's not your fault.
7. High expectations shape kids' lives.

5 Creating An Achieving Milleu Begin With The Picture

Victor Frankl is a concentration camp survivor. He said in a speech, "There is one reason I am here today. What kept me alive was you. I dreamed that someday I would be here, telling you how I, Victor Frankl, had survived the Nazi concentration camps. I've never given this speech before. But in my dreams, in my dreams, I have stood before you and said these words a thousand times."

What dreams do we create in the minds of kids? What images do we draw of their success?

The author of the classic book, *Psycho-Cybernetics*, Dr. Maxwell Maltx, wrote about the power of the mental image. He told of patients who came to see him for plastic surgery. After the tucks were taken or the nose made more appealing, the patients still felt unattractive. Why? Because although they had changed physically, their mental picture was the same.

THE GRADUATION SNAPSHOT

When I first started teaching all seniors, I quickly

realized that they had one major fear—graduation.

Now during the first week of school, I bring in a graduation program from the previous year. I deliver the following talk:

"Your name will be on this list. Your name is called and you walk proudly across the stage. The principal smiles and shakes your hand, then gives you the diploma. You look out into the audience and see your parents, friends and relatives, smiling and clapping for you."

Every year I take a roll of film at graduation to share with my new students during the beginning weeks of school. Throughout the year I give weekly reminders of their graduation.

THE TURN AROUND

One of my students made a D the first semester. By the start of the new semester, he did a complete turn around. When I noticed his improved grades and asked about his progress, he said that he had decided he needed to make some new friends. Two weeks before graduation he informed me that none of his old friends were getting diplomas.

I received the following end-of-the-year evaluation from him.

"I really would like to say thanks for making us meet each other because it made class fun. I wasn't afraid to ask questions and I felt comfortable in this class and not out of place.

"I liked this class because I had to work to be the best. I went from low scores to high just because I didn't want to watch my friends walk across the stage. I wanted to be there with them."

One year, in late May, one student asked if I would cheer for her when she crossed the stage. I told her I always bring my husband and friends as a cheering team. How could she doubt I wouldn't be there for her?

When we want to help kids achieve their goals, we need to first create clear pictures of those goals. Next, we need to give frequent reminders, encouragement and support. Someone once said that a goal is just a dream with a deadline.

And that dream has a picture attached.

1. See The Goal Achieved

I once worked with a school evaluation in a rural North Florida town. I met a dedicated English teacher whose kids had every reason not to be motivated. Their parents worked the orange groves. They were surrounded by poverty and although they were only an hour from the coast, most had never seen the Atlantic Ocean. Yet there was a sparkle and energy about the kids that one could almost touch.

Three of this teacher's students had won the top poetry awards in a statewide writing contest. How did he motivate them? When he read about the contest, he walked into his classroom and said, "Three winners are sitting in this room." Obviously, he was right.

It reminds me of the story of the old man praying to God to win the lottery. Finally he hears this deep, far-away voice that says, "Hey. Give me a break. Buy a ticket."

If we can get our kids to "buy the ticket," we are on the way to helping them achieve.

2. Become A Partner

One elementary teacher took a novel approach to the beginning of the year. She showed up in cowboy boots, jeans, vest and cowboy hat. She informed the kids they were to call her "Partner." That's what she was—a partner in their education. She used her clothes to create the powerful visual image of student and teacher working together to achieve success.

With the idea of partnering in mind, I've delivered the following talk to my students:

"I am your individual teacher. I teach the group, but I also teach you as a special member of my team. I can be the best teacher in the world and still fail as a teacher if I cannot get your cooperation to work toward your own success. I need you probably more than you need me. When you fail, then I have failed to teach. I don't like failure. I want to help you succeed because in doing that I can feel good about the way I'm spending my life. I cannot do it alone. I need your help."

3. Create A Working Environment

An artist friend of mine helps create convention displays for a small company. The company is very busy in the spring and fall, a time when most conventions are held. She hates her job the rest of the year because there is nothing to do. The money is good, but she wants to quit. The slow times drive her crazy.

Most people don't quit jobs where they feel needed and appreciated. They quit jobs where there is very little to do or where they are asked to look busy.

41

Paula Poundstone, a New York comedian who was a high school drop-out, said in an interview, "I couldn't rationalize going to school when I wasn't doing anything, and it wasn't any fun at all."

4. Set The Pace

On my first visit to New York City, I was most impressed with the energy level. I remember one Jamaican cab driver who drawled, "This is a fast town." That was an understatement.

In New York City, no one walks to work. They wear jogging shoes with their business suits and run. At intersections, they don't stand on the curb. They stand in the streets hunched down in racing positions as if waiting for the starting gun.

Several times, I caught myself moving quickly too. I was in Bloomingdales and found myself running up the escalator.

We have a tendency to pick up our energy and pace from those around us.

5. Create The Employed Atmosphere

What about the atmosphere in our classrooms? Do we create a working milleu? The best way to get kids working is to have them working immediately. I still remember a high school Spanish teacher who kept us busy from the moment the bell rang.

It is a credit to her good teaching that I still recall her class. She set up bookshelves on one side of the room. When we entered, we were to get just the Spanish book, paper and pen that we needed for class.

She made it quite clear that if we didn't have everything we needed, we would not be allowed to go to the bookshelves during class time. She taught until the bell rang. There was no wasted time.

6. Be Impatient With Getting Ready Time

Robert Updegraff had the following words about the benefits of impatience, "The world is cluttered up with unfinished business in the form of projects that might have been successful, if only at the tide point someone's patience had turned to active impatience."

We need a healthy impatience with "getting ready" time. Kids can avoid work by dawdling and hunting for papers, pencils, etc. The only answer is to have students start getting ready before the bell. Make it clear, like my Spanish teacher years ago, that when the bell rings, hunting time is over.

7. The Power of High Self-Esteem

The most important person in the classroom is not the student. The most important person in the classroom is the teacher.

A teacher with high self-esteem has the power to build the self-esteem of others. A teacher with low self-esteem is defeated before the first bell.

Build the self-esteem of one teacher and you help to build the self-image of thirty kids. The research shows that as a group, we don't nurture self-esteem in one another.

I once attended a meeting with a group of sales people from a large paper manufacturing firm. When I walked into the room, the smiles, energy and enthusiasm were incredible.

Everyone was on a first-name basis including the vice-president and president. The atmosphere was friendly, relaxed and informal.

How different from some faculty meetings I have attended. The next time you are in a large group meeting of teachers, check out the atmosphere. Is the group smiling or depressed, and what is your contribution?

8. Build Self-Esteem. Begin At Home

Teaching alone won't build our self-esteem, because no job can fill all our needs. The moment we expect it to, is the moment we fail.

You and I have self-worth, not because we teach or because we are good in our profession. *We have self-worth because we exist. Our existence alone makes us valuable and important.*

One of my colleagues has a coffee cup with the message, "Some people teach, others choose less significant work."

I have participated as a member of school evaluation teams. We usually work in a group of twenty-five teachers and administrators. Our visit begins with an evening dinner. During this time the visiting team is introduced to the faculty. The differences in teachers' attitude toward the subjects and level of kids they work with are remarkable.

The teacher who says, "I teach chem study," or, "I teach calculus," expresses pride and conviction. But it doesn't hold true for all teachers.

When I hear, "I teach basic skills," or, "I teach low level math," a lower, almost apologetic tone of voice is used. We need to have our best teachers in classes where kids need the most work. And why should one course or ability level reflect our intelligence or confidence?

A professor at Iowa State University did some research concerning teacher self-esteem. The work involved over one thousand teachers in twenty-three Iowa high schools.

It was discovered that the ability level of the students affected the teachers' job satisfaction. Teachers who taught

44

low-ability students, ranked themselves lower in self-esteem than those teachers with average or high ability students. What does this mean for us? If we teach low level kids, we'd better be stock-piling our self-esteem in some other area of our lives or we'll be in trouble.

Students are great readers of our body language and our attitude. So the next time we are introducing ourselves, let's be aware of the hidden message behind our words.

9. How Powerful Is The Label?

My job as a visiting team member was to evaluate the high school's English program. In this North Florida school, I was looking for a specific room number and entered what I thought was the right classroom. I sat down in the back of the room.

Although the class has half over, there was a great deal of confusion as to what the students were supposed to be doing. Two or three wandered around the room aimlessly. A few worked quietly at their desks. The moment I entered, kids shouted things like, "We have a visitor," and, "What's your name?", etc.

The teacher was helping someone near the front of the room. I leaned over to the student next to me and whispered, "What class is this anyway?" He looked up and said, "Why, this is the dummy class. Can't you tell?"

10. One Label Per Customer

The student is our customer. When we label our customers, we create problems. When we call kids "gifted" and put them in a separate room with only "bright" kids, we set up an atmosphere for success. When we put only "low achieving" kids together, we set up an atmosphere for failure. We need to pull away from labeling everyone's mentality. It's bringing down the esteem of our valued students, and lowering ours as well.

11. Suspend Disbelief

Samuel Coleridge in the preface to his long poem *The Rhyme of the Ancient Mariner* describes the willing suspension of disbelief.

He explains to the reader that in order to enjoy the poem he/she must suspend disbelief. An attitude that says, "This could never happen in real life," will interfere with the enjoyment of his narrative.

Sometimes we may hear a good teaching idea or technique from a colleague and the first words we say are, "Well that worked for you, but it won't work in my classes." That is negative thinking. How much better to say, "Perhaps it will work for me. I'll try it."

I had a so called "low ability" class a few years ago that gave me much trouble. I tried an experiment with them that proved to be most successful.

We divided into teams of two and did a research paper. Many in the group had never been to the library. Few knew how to do research and assimilate information. Managing their behavior in the library wasn't easy. Because they were often suspended, some missed school on a regular basis.

I sometimes had to read and translate the material. But since the students chose their topics (teenage gangs, cocaine) they at least were researching something they were interested in.

The last part of the assignment was for the students to stand in teams of two in front of the room, become the experts and teach the class on the subject of their papers.

They were wonderful. The experiment was the turning point in their behavior.

46

If I hadn't been willing to try team research papers or if I had doubted they could ever succeed, we would have both been denied the opportunity to achieve.

Sometimes the willing suspension of disbelief gives us all the courage to try.

12. Show Your Good Face

A pessimist never suspends doubts. A pessimist smells the roses and asks, "Where's the funeral?" Most pessimists I know don't call themselves pessimists, they call themselves realists. But nothing is ever realistic or unrealistic. Just like the student in the "dummy class," we create our own reality from the cues around us.

Someone once said that an optimist fails as often as a pessimist, but that the optimist has a lot more fun. An optimist expects to succeed. Baseball scouts call the look that radiates from the optimist the "good face." It is a sense of confidence that top performers seem to possess. Kids deserve to see our good face. Are you showing your good face today?

SUMMARY:

1. Create the picture.
2. Become a partner.
3. Create the employed atmosphere.
4. Build your self-esteem.
5. Be aware of labels.
6. Suspend disbelief.
7. Show your good face.

---

6 Making Changes: Magic Cards

A few years ago two friends of mine opened a retail store. They sold Mexican trinkets and cotton sweaters. The sweaters sold immediately. They didn't try harder to sell Mexican souvenirs. No, they bought more cotton sweaters and casual clothes. They learned early to give the customer what the customer wanted.

They now own about twenty-five stores throughout the country and are busy building more. In addition to being creative and hard-working, they listened to the marketplace. They listened to their customers.

They didn't try to do the impossible by attempting to change the customer's mind. Unfortunately for our students, we don't always follow this same logic in the classroom.

When my friends adjusted the merchandise, they met the needs of their customers. Similarly, we need to adjust our motivation techniques to meet the needs of our students, our customers.

The Student Is The Customer

The young person in my classroom is both the client and the customer. He consumes what I teach. Indirectly, he pays my salary.

Fill The Customer's Needs

We can receive everything we need simply by helping kids attain what they need, first. We cannot predict their wants in advance. We begin by asking and being willing to listen to their responses.

What Do Kids Really Need?

1. They need to belong to the group.
2. They need to feel accepted.
3. They need to be recognized.
4. They need to feel successful.

What About The Teacher?

We would like the kids' confidence but not necessarily their friendship. They have plenty of friends. We need their respect. We need to like children but must not have an urgent need to be liked by them every minute of the day.

THIS SPECIAL RELATIONSHIP

The student/teacher relationship is like a love relationship. Sometimes in a love relationship we expect our loved one to provide us with what we need without our having to ask. Yet asking for what we need, sure makes life easier.

The student/teacher relationship is also unique in that it is forever. I was attending a convention and met a lovely woman from Miami who was friends with my eighth grade English teacher.

This was the English teacher everyone hoped to have. She was the first teacher to ask me to write creatively. We not only wrote poetry, but we published our works in a small class magazine. I still remember her and she is still my teacher.

Our special relationship is vital for motivation. I may know my students' general needs, but I can only discover their specific needs by asking them. Using magic cards is the answer.

I call them magic cards because they have the power to change and improve relationships.

THE TEACHER'S REPORT CARD

The magic card is an evaluation of the teacher and the class. To help guide the students, write the following on the board or overhead:

What do you love about this class?
What do you hate about this class?
What one thing would you like to see changed?

Explaining Magic Cards

"I've given each one of you an index card. This is a magic card almost like a report card for me, your teacher. The principal comes into this classroom twice a year to evaluate me. But you are the ones who know me best, and you are never asked.

"I'm asking now. I want your thoughts and feelings. I'm not concerned with proper grammar or handwriting. I simply am looking for ways I can improve as your teacher. I'm looking for honesty.

"I'm not perfect. The minute I become perfect, you'll be in big trouble. Right now, you're safe. You have the right to make mistakes and so do I. Just because I've taught a number of years, doesn't mean I do everything correctly. I make mistakes, too.

"I'm still growing and hopefully becoming a better teacher each year, but I can't do it alone. I need your help."

After The Instructions

This is an individual assignment that takes about ten minutes or less. Instead of collecting cards yourself, have students place them on a shelf. One friend of mine has students write magic cards on the day she knows a substitute will be teaching. That works, too.

The Reaction

Be prepared for the students' reactions. Many will rub their hands together in glee. Others will be suspicious. Since they aren't used to being honest with their teachers, at first they might be afraid to share their feelings. An encouraging attitude is your best defense.

Magic Card Warning

Try this activity on a day when you're feeling good about yourself. Don't do it on a day you're in a bad mood. It takes courage and confidence to ask kids to evaluate us. Only the teacher with high self-esteem will attempt it.

How often should it be done? At least four times a year. Do a card two to three weeks after the opening of school. Do a second in late October. A third one in late January and a fourth in March.

Second semester is always a good time because if done early enough, you can still make changes before the end of the year. May is the worst time to do a magic card. If you decide to do one in June, vary the questions. Ask students what they enjoyed most this year, and what changes would help next year's students succeed.

Interpretation Of Cards

I guarantee that these cards will make fascinating reading. Kids can be painfully honest and wonderfully sincere.

Vicious Cards

You might receive a few. Hopefully not many. I have cynics in my classes too. Winning over every child is impossible.

Ignore the cynic. Try not to take their remarks personally. Instead, concentrate on the next category.

Pattern Cards

These cards have a similar message and repeat a suggestion for my improvement. One year I received cards that said, "You speak too fast," and, "When you lecture, I can't write notes." The next day I shared this information and we worked out a solution. Everytime I was talking too quickly, they were to raise their hands.

My students now tell me to slow down, and it makes me a more effective teacher.

When you get three to five cards with a specific complaint, you might have an area that needs improvement.

The Benefits

Magic cards create an atmosphere of trust. Kids know that you listen.

A second advantage is what I call positive brain-washing. I read aloud the positive cards that point out good things about my teaching or personality.

I also write a magic card and read it aloud the next day. By doing this, I'm letting students know that together we can make changes.

Evaluation Cards: Reality Checks

The kindergarten teacher was feeling quite proud of her young students. They had learned to recite their home addresses. As part of the safety lesson, she also taught them the importance of dialing 911 in an emergency.

The children were busy singing "911, 911" when one little boy brought the lesson to an abrupt reality halt. He raised his hand and said, "I'd feel lots better if I knew what a nine looked like."

Kids can memorize and dictate back to us anything we wish to teach. But the training we give doesn't mean a great deal until it transfers to the real world.

Does Your Teaching Transfer?

One way to check on this transfer to reality is to ask our experts, our students. If you teach tenth grade, simply visit with a few former students and ask them what has helped them from your course.

One of my students became a successful actor. When he stopped by the school for a visit, I asked what had helped him about our eighth grade class. He said that I had taught him how to breathe properly using his diaphragm, and that had been most useful for him.

Kids will remember the skill they use over and over again. Yet, we don't have to wait years to get this valuable feedback.

Use Daily, Weekly Checks

At the end of a project or three-day unit, we can ask kids what they hated, loved, and learned. A good end of the class activity is to simply ask students, "What did you learn?" or, "What did you re-learn?"

Listening to students' responses is not just an excellent review, but a good way to check our progress too.

I received a comment from a senior I will never forget. We had just finished writing team research papers. My students worked with partners through note cards, rough and final drafts. Then, they presented the information to the class.

When one team, Frank and Sarah, stood to give their talk, it was obvious that Sarah had done the work. Her answer for the evaluation question, "What did I learn?" was "I learned how to pick my friends."

Magic cards along with daily checks and frequent evaluations all help to make us better teachers. When we improve our teaching skills, our job becomes easier. We work smarter.

Next we'll talk about some methods that work to reach the resistant kids in our classes.

SUMMARY:

1. **Magic cards build trust and create change.**
2. **The student is the customer. Fill the customer's needs.**
3. **Kids need to belong, to be accepted, to be recognized and to be successful.**
4. **The teacher/student relationship is like a love relationship.**
5. **High self-esteem teachers use magic cards.**
6. **Daily and weekly evaluations are reality checks.**

7 *Winning Over Resistant Kids*

I grew up with three brothers. We all hated vegetables, especially the ones that showed up like clockwork on our dinner plates.

Brussel sprouts were the worst. We called them green meatballs. Our parents pleaded with us, "Just try them this once."

"But we tried them last week, and we didn't like them."

"Makes no difference. This time, you'll like them." Then came the bribe. "Finish your plate and you get key lime pie." That's all the incentive I needed. I swallowed them whole. But my brother Bill had a different way of coping.

He'd place all three brussel sprouts into his left cheek. Dad would scold, "Bill, chew your food." And looking a lot like George Carlin, he'd say, "I am chewing my food."

Then he'd mumble, "I need more milk," and he'd bolt for the trash can.

Just like my brother, kids in a classroom have

various ways of rejecting our attempts at motivation. It helps to remember that we don't have to eliminate all resistance to win the class.

When I first began teaching, I made that mistake. I thought I could coerce kids into my way of thinking. I naturally knew what was right for them. I was the adult.

I soon discovered that kids resist. They use subterfuge. They'd forget homework and leave pencils, papers and books at home.

My plans failed because instead of facing and acknowledging resistance, I fought it. Understanding and dealing with resistance is a big hurdle. We need to meet it with a frontal attack.

In this chapter we will discuss the Six-Step Resistance Plan. Then we will help increase students' motivation by answering the three questions kids ask most often.

SIX-STEP RESISTANCE PLAN

1. Get The Negative First

One of my toughest assignments is getting kids interested in writing poetry. The average high school student grumbles and complains when told, "We'll be writing poems today."

First, clear the air of the negative feelings. Ask students: "Tell me everything you hate about poetry." I get an immediate response. I might get one student who says, "I don't know. I kind of like poetry." Good, I've won some support.

2. Accept The Student's Viewpoint

I agree with some of the comments. My response is: "You are right. Poetry can be confusing and difficult to understand." Now students are shaking their heads. That helps win cooperation.

3. Replace Resistance

We need to replace resistance with thoughts of recognition, prestige, pleasure or payment. While they are still shaking their heads, I become the sales person.

"It's wonderful to make an 'A' especially for a short, easy assignment, isn't it? How would you like to earn not just an 'A' but gain 100 points? That will be a real boost to your average."

To make the "payment" of the "A" grade effective, the papers need to be resumed the next day.

4. Sell The Assignment

Many times kids will refuse to do an assignment because they fear failing. That's why I make poetry writing "fail proof." All poems will get the "A" regardless of their quality.

5. Establish Clear, Reachable Deadlines

When I give assignments like poetry writing, I know the students can complete the work by the end of the period. When the bell rings, I stand at the door and collect papers. It gives me another chance to motivate. I use their names and thank students as they leave.

6. Follow-Up

Before the next day, I'll quickly read over the poems marking good lines, clever titles and innovative phrases. At the beginning of the next class, students are greeted with the following: "In my hands are some of the best poems I've ever read. Now I'll be sharing some of these with you." I'll read aloud parts of the poems with comments like, "This is a great title," or, "Listen to this clever last line."

This six-step resistance plan works regardless of the level of your students. Even when students are indifferent about earning 100 points, they still crave recognition and prestige. Why not have them write their names on the chalkboard? The main point is to give them a reward that matches their maturity.

IMPROVEMENT THROUGH ENCOURAGEMENT

Sometimes it's to our advantage to stretch the truth. I do know that most of the students will improve—and they will improve because they hear good poetry and because they've been encouraged by a no-fail environment.

Mark the papers and record the grades. There may be a student or two who didn't turn in a poem. Any poem that comes in a day late receives 90 points.

The other advantage to this method is that I've had students hear the poems and ask to take theirs home to improve them. Now that's what motivation is all about. Getting kids to be self-starters.

The Magic of Providing Feedback

The authors of *The One-Minute Manager* call feedback the breakfast of champions. I remember the frustration of college classes, where the only grade I received for a course was the final exam. I sometimes waited weeks for the exam results.

It's better to give papers back the next day with one or two skills graded, than to hold papers for a week and lose the momentum.

Maybe what is needed is a stamp that says, "All the errors in this paper haven't been found." Keeping papers too long is detrimental for motivation.

Now that we have overcome some resistance, let's next motivate kids by answering the questions they most want answered.

Number 1 most asked question

What Are We Doing Today?

We are not being paid to repeat ourselves end-lessly. Since this is the number one question kids want answered on a daily basis, let's make the answer easy.

Point to the board where you've written the day's lesson plan in four or five short phrases. Then say, "That."

Number 2 most asked question

What'd We Do Yesterday?

Let's take the mystery out of make-up work. Put the burden for make-up work back on the shoulders of the student.

How to let go
of the omnipotent expert role

When a kid is absent, he comes into class the next day, heads directly for the teacher and asks about make-up work. What could be wrong with that? Everything.

To begin with, it took you fifty-five minutes to teach the assignment. Now you're being asked to give a brief summary in the minute or two before class starts. Your mind is spinning with thoughts of today's plans.

It's a no-win situation. What if you leave out some important information? The student can always retaliate with, "But you didn't tell me that." And of course he'll be right.

Managing make-up work
so it doesn't make us mad

Phone Mates

The best way to manage make-up work is to assign

phone mates. During the first week of school, ask students to select two other classmates and share telephone numbers. When absent, students call a phone mate to get the missed assignments. Two numbers are better than one just in case a line is busy, or the phone mate was absent as well.

When kids return to class, they have an idea of the missed work. Next, they check the Make-Up Log.

Make-Up Log

The Make-Up Log is a spiral notebook. One student per week writes today's date plus two sentences about the assignments.

If students are absent Monday and return to school Tuesday, they read the assignments from the Make-Up Log. If there are questions, they see the expert who wrote the sentences or refer to the Make-Up Folder.

The Make-Up Folder

This is a bright red folder that contains all handouts and ditto material. It's convenient when kids "lose" weekly assignments, homework schedules, etc. It also reinforces the information in the Make-Up Log.

Make Make-Up Work Accessible

Keep the Make-Up Log and Make-Up Folder on a table that is easily reached. When do students retrieve this information? During the few minutes before class starts.

Do kids still try to put me in the role of omnipotent expert? Sure they do. Now I respond by pointing to the table that holds the information they need and say simply, "There's your make-up work."

My students also know that I am available for brief conferences during the last five minutes of class time.

How Am I Doing?

Kids deserve to get their grades once a week or every other week. Some of us get overly protective of the gradebook. Giving out grades can be a tremendous motivator.

One tightly run high school in my county has set aside every other Wednesday as the day teachers give grade averages. The students bring in a special notebook. The averages are recorded and carried home to parents. The results? Over a two-year period this school has the lowest failure rate in the county.

Too much of a burden on the teacher? Perhaps. I have found the computer to be invaluable for giving weekly grades. If it helps get work turned in and kids succeeding, then it's a valuable use of my time.

Now that we've reduced resistance and motivated our students with answers, we'll look at ways to encourage good behavior.

SUMMARY: *The Six-Step Resistance Plan:*	1. Get negative first. 2. Accept their viewpoint. 3. Replace resistance. 4. Sell assignment. 5. Establish deadlines. 6. Follow-up

ANSWER KIDS' QUESTIONS:

What are we doing?
What'd we do yesterday?
How am I doing today?

Discipline Strategies For Managing The Bad, Bored And Belligerent

8

I used to believe that if I were doing a good job as a teacher, I could eliminate most discipline problems. I still believe that to a point.

Kids who are feeling successful, who are feeling that the work being done in the classroom is meaningful and important to them, don't usually tear the room down.

After twenty years of classroom teaching, I have developed some techniques that work well. I have borrowed my ideas from a variety of sources. One of the richest sources we have is one another. I have gained valuable ideas from good teachers, good teachers like you.

Sometimes discipline techniques fail because we expect too much. We hope that one plan, one consult-

ant, one book will wave the magician's wand over all our problems.

It just won't happen.

These techniques might work for you, sometimes, but not everytime. Factors like the hour of the day, the mood we are in or the age/maturity of our students must be considered. The variables can be limitless.

I picked up a list of educational books and one title intrigued me. It was something like *Discipline: 399 Problems and Solutions*. The title alone made me tired.

If I did somehow manage to get through the book, how could I possibly remember all the remedies?

WHAT BEHAVIOR CAN I CONTROL?

The only behavior I can change and control is my own. I can alter my emotional reaction to students' misbehavior. I can create a climate in the classroom where most students want to behave. I can reward appropriate behavior. But I cannot do the impossible of changing someone else's behavior.

I offer you my mixed assortment of discipline tips in the hopes that you may find a few that will be workable in your classroom.

1. Corrections versus Emotional Outbursts

There is a big difference between an emotional outburst and a correction. One is upsetting and not conducive to respect. The other is constructive, calming and builds respect.

An emotional outburst . . .

interrupts the teaching.
combines sarcasm and threats.
humiliates and destroys confidence.

leaves us feeling discouraged.
is usually given while standing.

A correction ...

doesn't interrupt the teaching.
is given in a soft, calm voice.
is handled in a semi-private or a private setting.
builds initiative and encourages new effort.
leaves the student willing to improve.
is best accomplished while seated.

Corrections work to our advantage. A seated position is recommended because we have the most resistance while standing. The major difference between the two approaches is that during a correction the teacher is in control of his/ her behavior.

Think back to your own recent discipline problems. Were you using corrections or emotional outbursts?

2. Catch Kids Behaving

We discussed complimenting kids in the previous chapter. We can also compliment a class on behavior. Open a class with, "I'm so pleased that you have read the instructions on the board and have your books open to page seventy. I appreciate the fact that you are ready to work in here. I notice that many of you have paper and pencil handy. That is a wonderful way to be prepared to start the day."

I compliment attendance. Most of my high school students drive or have access to a car. The eight-foot fence around the school and the double stainless steel gates on the parking lot entrance are not going to keep anyone on campus.

Liking or at least being able to tolerate school and enjoying the other kids in the class might help. Kids know that if they don't show up not only will I notice, but so will their teammates. A classroom of students who care about one another makes a difference.

A colleague in my department remarked, "The kids don't want to work; they just want to show up." If I can get kids to show up, I've won eighty percent of the battle. So I compliment attendance because the opportunity to skip is there.

Woody Allen once said, "Most of life is just showing up." Let's get kids attending, and we are well on the way to teaching them something.

Major Discipline Problems

On the secondary level, in grades six through twelve, skipping school and not turning work in are two major discipline problems.

One year in May, I noticed that two fair-skinned girls came to our sixth-hour class with progressively better tans. I mentioned to one girl that it looked like she had been to the beach. And she said, "Yes. Karen and I are skipping the first three periods and getting some sun."

Then I asked her why she and her friend didn't just stay at the beach all day. She said that she couldn't afford to miss my class. "We do too much work in here. If I started skipping sixth hour, I'd never get caught up."

These two young ladies had figured out what classes they could afford to miss. A student conference was the logical consequence to correct the behavior.

The Student Conference

The student conference is not a conversation. It is a one- to two-minute reprimand that lets the young person know that you are not happy with the misbehavior.

It needs to be done in a semi-private or private setting. Finding an appropriate place for a conference is difficult in a crowded school, but I have used an empty classroom or the library.

I've also created a quiet corner in the back of my room. It consists of two overstuffed chairs. I use this area during the last five minutes of the period while my students are talking quietly. I can still keep my eyes on the class, yet it offers a semi-private setting.

You will need to decide in advance the behavior that needs correcting. You can only reprimand one behavior per conference.

Pull up a chair and sit close. Look the student directly in the eye and say:

Step 1—State The Way You Feel

"I feel badly (angry, sad, hurt, disappointed, etc.) when you . . .

Step 2—State The Misbehavior

Use simple terms. Be direct.

Step 3—Wait.

Look directly at the student and be sure your facial expression matches your mood. Count fifteen seconds silently to let the student feel your emotions.

Step 4—Expect It Not To Recur. End With A Closing Positive Statement

Continue with, "Now that you know how I feel, I'm sure that won't happen again. I like your work (talents, enthusiasm, humor, insights, art, etc.)." Always end with a sincere compliment.

Step 5—Thank The Student. Use His/Her Name

"I appreciate, Cheryl, your staying after school. Thank you."

This two-minute conference works because the teacher is calm and collected. We are not criticizing or berating. We are simply sharing our feelings. It is amazing how good I feel after a reprimand conference. The feeling is mutual. I've had students thank me. I think they, too, are relieved.

HANDLING THE MINOR HASSLES

Most of our discipline problems involve minor aggravations. These include coming to class late, non-stop chatter, forgetting homework and refusing to complete assignments on time. These small annoyances fill our day, distract us from the real job of teaching and turn our hair gray.

1. Make Sure Assignments Are Clear

Sometimes what we say is not what the students hear. It is best to have a student rephrase the assignment.

After giving an assignment, try this: "I've just walked into the room. I have no idea what is going on. Would one of you please tell me what *I* should be doing?"

I am sometimes amazed at the discrepancy between what I thought I said and what the students heard. This double check is valuable. It eliminates much of the talk that occurs after an assignment because kids know what is expected.

2. Give Kids Permission To Talk

Legal talking is done at your convenience. During the last ten minutes, tell students they will review the material. Then go around the room and have students say, "I learned . . ." Or "I re-learned. . ." Each learner gets a chance to say something productive which helps to review and rehash the material you have just taught.

Some days I start my review early because the room needs to be re-arranged or materials need to be put away.

Bribes work well, too. I've told my kids, "We have a specific amount of work that must be done today. If we can all cooperate and get the assignments completed, then I'll give you the last five minutes of the period to talk." Just knowing that they will have a chance to share a few ideas with one another helps to eliminate the chatter.

The $1,000 Discipline Tip

Most of the time kids get into trouble for talking when they should be working. This technique allows us to correct the minor misbehavior in a quiet way that maintains the dignity of our very important client.

Let us set the scene. Students are answering study questions in teams of two. You are answering individual questions and moving throughout the room.

You notice David. He is shifting through baseball cards. His science text is closed, his notebook paper is blank, and he is talking with the student who sits in front of him.

Since David is in the back corner of the room and you are in the front helping another student, you realize you won't be able to get to him right away.

Step 1:
Stare at David. You might be able to catch his eyes and your scowl could be enough incentive to get him back to work.

Step 2:
Walk over to David. It helps to be physically close.

Put your hand on his desk or shoulder.

Step 3:
Use his name and give a direct command. "David, do your study questions."

Step 4:
Wait, patiently. Be silent. This is the most difficult part. Court thirty seconds but say nothing. Continue to stand next to his desk. Wait for him to put aside the baseball cards and open his text. Your physical presence is the key to his getting back on track.

Step 5:
Say, "Thank you, David." Always say "thank you" and use the student's name. Why? Because you want him to know that you are appreciative of his efforts.

Many years ago, I first saw this technique demonstrated in a workshop by Dr. Harry Wong, an educational consultant and expert teacher from California. It is a simple, effective tool for correcting misbehavior.

Just like anything else, it may take several attempts before you feel comfortable with the technique. It is powerful not only because it works, but because it creates a positive feeling between teacher and student.

I have seen it used with elementary as well as high school students. I am sometimes pleasantly surprised when I have thanked the student and he/she says, "You are welcome, Mrs. Fuery."

A Word About Touch

When you use this discipline technique, you have a choice. You may either touch the student lightly on the shoulder, or place the palm of your hand on his/her desk. If you question whether to touch or not, perhaps it would be best not to touch.

I have reached the age where I could be the mother of my students. If I can't touch kids, then I can't teach them. Touching is a natural expression of my personality.

However, I also respect the student who does not like to be touched. Junior high kids will even brush off the touch of someone they don't know or don't like. Physical contact needs to be used with discretion. For some of our kids, the only touch they know is the one done in anger.

I have been in a conference with students who when touched on a shoulder or forearm, relaxed. Touch can be a powerful motivator and soother of nerves. Use touch when you feel it is appropriate.

3. Weekly Study Sessions

I rarely fail a student who attempts the work. Kids who fail my classes, and they are a very small percentage, generally don't turn work in. They fail by default.

Weekly detentions are one answer. Here's how it works. Leslie doesn't turn in a social studies paper due on Thursday. I see her fifth hour, and on Friday the paper is still missing. I remind her to turn the paper in late or risk staying after school on Tuesday (my detention day).

If the paper is turned in before Tuesday, Leslie won't have to serve a detention. The detention is basically a study period to get the assignments finished. Most of my students work after school and evenings. Many times just the threat of a detention gets the work in.

But what about kids who skip the detention? I call home. I may even have a counselor call and set up a conference with the parent.

Detentions become a study hall for kids who have difficulty planning their time. I provide a quiet place to work. As soon as the work is completed, they can leave. They can avoid the detention all together by showing up with assignment in hand.

If a student fails three quizzes in a row, I assign a detention to discover the cause. It could be that the individual isn't reading the required novel. Then the detention provides a quiet place for reading.

I don't want kids failing my class. Detentions give me a little extra time to work with students and hopefully help them succeed.

4. The 'Time Out' Conduct Report

Many schools have set up "time out" areas where kids who continually disturb the class can go. I think the idea of a "time out" room is wonderful for one reason. It gives the teacher a day's break from the student.

Sometimes I wonder how much thinking the student does about his/her misbehavior. At the end of this book, you will find a time out conduct report.

When you send a student from the classroom, before you see them again, have them fill out this report.

What If There Is No Time Out Room?

If your school does not have a time out room, there is a solution. Simply send the kid to another teacher's classroom, preferably one where the disrupting student does not know lots of other kids.

When I taught middle school, I sent eighth graders into sixth grade classes. I made prior arrangements with the sixth grade teacher.

When my student appeared at the other teacher's doorway, she indicated a chair and told the student that as soon as the form was completed, he/she could leave.

The form took about ten minutes and gave me a

chance to plan my next discipline strategy.

5. Calling Home

When we have a problem with a student who refuses to complete the assignments or who disrupts a class, we hesitate to call home. Usually we make every effort to talk with the student first.

It has been said that we should never work alone. Let kids know in advance that if they fail to turn in work or if they create havoc in the classroom, we will call their parents.

Patents hold all kinds of power. Kids really don't want their parents to know what is happening in school. *I* think sometimes we don't call home for help because we are intimidated by the parent's position in the community.

One year, I had the daughter of an assistant superintendent. I discovered that she had skipped my class for two days. I felt awkward calling the mother in the county office and reporting the offense.

The assistant superintendent was cordial and thanked me.

The girl's attendance improved. I could not know in advance the mother's reaction to my calling. I simply had to call and tell her what was happening in school.

Over the years, I have called many, many parents. It is my best PR tool. It lets kids and the community know that we care. The best advertising is a satisfied customer. Calling home creates satisfied customers.

By calling home in time, when the parents' influence can affect a student's performance, we do both child and parent a favor. And one warning: Don't assume automatically that the parents don't care. That's an excuse for not calling. I've found that parents are sometimes intimidated by teachers. Here are some suggestions to make calling home easier.

The Calling Home Technique

1. *Call between six and seven p.m.*
2. *Keep your conversation short*
3. *Identify yourself immediately*—"This is Carol Fuery. I teach your son Chris. He is in my fourth hour math class. I find that he has not turned in the last four homework papers. This will affect his grade. I wonder if you might check with him about completing those assignments." Continue with, "I have five other parents I need to call tonight . . . Thank you for your help."
4. *Always thank the parent*—End the conversation quickly. You don't want a five-year history on why Chris doesn't like math. If the parent needs to talk with you, schedule a time to meet. Don't let this telephone call become a "my son hates math because of his second grade teacher. . ." conversation.

I rely on the student underground. I try to call about five parents a week. Some weeks I might need to call ten, but only reach three or four. That is all right. The student underground gets the word out. "She's calling home," and late papers are turned in.

As my own incentive, I pour myself a half of glass of wine. Before I dial the first parent, I place the wine in the freezer.

I give myself ten to fifteen minutes. Wine doesn't take that long to get really cold. When I'm through calling home, I can relax, knowing I've done the best I could for the kids under my care.

Effective discipline means management of our emotions and our behavior. We can't change kids. We can change our reaction to their misbehavior.

I am sure that over the years you have developed your own special techniques for handling student misbehavior. You are the champion in your situation. If I have been able to provide one new suggestion, that will be enough.

Next we'll discuss how to be our most encouraging selves.

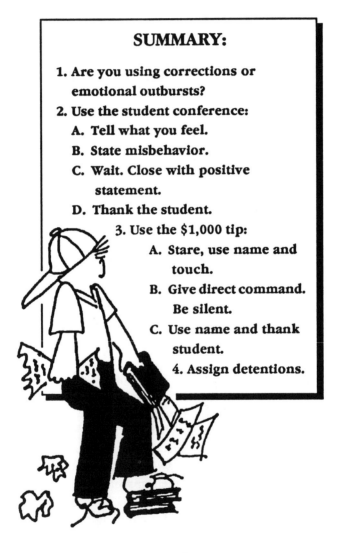

SUMMARY:

1. Are you using corrections or emotional outbursts?
2. Use the student conference:
   A. Tell what you feel.
   B. State misbehavior.
   C. Wait. Close with positive statement.
   D. Thank the student.
      3. Use the $1,000 tip:
         A. Stare, use name and touch.
         B. Give direct command. Be silent.
         C. Use name and thank student.
         4. Assign detentions.

9 *The Language of Encouragement*

I took a close friend of mine shopping. Sue had overcome a major illness and recently had difficulty managing her junior high classes. My plan was to take her to lunch, do some shopping and in general try to help her feel a little better about herself.

We went into a popular women's clothing store that does a big business mostly because they take a personal interest in their customers.

The moment we entered the shop, the sales woman introduced herself as Kate. She asked our names. Within ten minutes, Sue was wearing a new dress.

The entire time Kate gave words of encouragement like, "That color pink looks wonderful against your skin. The skirt is a good cut. Here, try this scarf and see if you like it better."

My friend left the store with a new ensemble and a new outlook. She bought her clothes as a result of a good sales person but also because she was given encouragement to buy. It wasn't just a sales pitch.

The clerk had selected a suitable outfit. There was

a sincerity and enthusiasm on the part of the sales team.

When a customer leaves a store looking good and feeling good, they become walking billboards. Satisfied customers advertise stores in ways that huge budgets can't.

The same holds true for kids in our classrooms. Students who are succeeding spread the good word throughout the school and into the community.

I am amazed at the popularity of the bumper stickers that I see on cars around the county that say, "My child is an honor student at Lake Park Middle School." That's advertising for the world to see.

Tom Peters, co-author of *In Search of Excellence,* believes that the "customer relationship is everything in every business." He advises business owners to "think relationship or go broke." That is also true of kids in our classes. Students who we reach and teach become well-serviced consumers. They consume what we offer and become our appreciating assets.

A VOTE FOR TEACHER

I had the opportunity to interview a superintendent in a rural county about sixty miles from my home. This lovely woman was about fifty-five years old. She had lived in the area most of her life. She was a junior high teacher, principal, county level administrator and now voted by the community to be their superintendent.

She credited her achievements with her successful teaching. She said, "I was voted in by my former students. I taught the contingency." Her advice to teachers was, "Treat students with courtesy and respect. Then you will own the community. And you may be alone."

TEACHER AS A SALESPERSON

When I went into teaching over eighteen years ago I failed to recognize that I went into sales. But it soon became evident to me that if I could encourage kids to buy into my program, philosophy, style of teaching . . . then I had a chance at helping them grow. If I failed to win my customer, then all my good teaching was wasted effort.

Just like my friend Sue who needed encouragement to purchase the outfit that was best for her, kids in our classrooms need constant encouragement do to what's best for them.

PERSONAL ATTENTION THROUGH TOUCH

Several years ago a popular bumper sticker read, "Have you hugged your kids today?" Hugs can work miracles. A hug can lift a depression, make us feel less tired and more vibrant.

Yet we have an excessive fear about touching. A large school district in Florida warned teachers at the beginning of the school year that touching was forbidden. I couldn't teach kids if I couldn't touch kids.

TOUCHING REGULATIONS

Hugging is a natural expression of sincere emotion that can only happen in an atmosphere of trust. It helps to get the other person's permission. Even very small youngsters may equate touch with punishment. So, go slowly at first.

The very children we overlook or avoid hugging are probably the ones who need attention the most. A friend of mine related a story that happened in her eleventh grade social studies class. The students were assigned to give individual reports in the front of the room.

Most of the students had little experience in speaking before the class. Before their talk began, the teacher touched each student lightly on the shoulder. The pat on the shoulder was optional.

Because of this light touch on the shoulder, most students took a deep breath and really relaxed before speaking.

One young man had given her a rough time for the past three weeks. His father had left his mother, and he was having a difficult time coping with the loss. He was determined to take out his anger and frustration on others in the class.

It was Jody's turn to speak. Mrs. Koss was standing near the podium when an aide from the office came in to talk with her. She completely forgot about touching Jody. After the aide left, she said to him, "Well, I guess now we're ready to begin."

Jody said, "But Mrs. Koss, aren't you forgetting something?" And then she remembered. "You're right. I am forgetting something important."

She stood facing the class and put her arm around the boy's shoulder, and said, "Don't we make a great mother/ son combination?"

It was a sincere, spontaneous remark.

That little touch and attention became the turning point for Jody. My friend reported weeks later that his friendliness and enthusiasm had returned.

THE AVENUE FOR PRAISE: A FOOTPATH OR FREEWAY

Touching with words, words of encouragement and praise give us all the strength to keep working when things get tough. We might think we are being encouraging, but unless we say the words, kids won't always get the message. Let's vocalize our feelings.

Group Praise That Motivates

This is my favorite class.
This is a first class class.
I like being here with you.
I am pleased with the progress this class has made.
As a group, you are
   . . . doing a good job and should feel proud.
   . . . doing everything right.
   . . . showing lots of improvement.
   . . . displaying high energy. . . I appreciate you.

Individual Praise That Motivates

I like you.
You've got your brain in gear.
Marvelous, I think you've got it now.
You are on the right track.
That's the right way to do it.
Great. I never would have thought of that.
Your work is . . . super, outstanding, fantastic.
That's quite an improvement.
Congratulations. That's the best you've ever done.
You've figured that out quickly.
You make my job easy.

APPEARING ENCOURAGING TO KIDS

The following letter came from a second year band

teacher in Texas.

"My first year of teaching has been filled with many trials and tribulations, many I caused. Students thought of me as a cold and uncaring person.

"Many of the students liked the progress the bands were making but did not like the actual class. As a result, I lost several good students and more were on their way out.

"The week before Thanksgiving, ten students decided to try to quit. I was given a meeting with both the principal and the superintendent. They took the time to explain that the kids liked what they were learning in class, but that they did not feel I 'cared' about them as students.

"I almost quit my job at that point. The principal explained that I appeared negative. I almost could not believe it! I knew that I was rarely positive, but . . . they informed me that I needed to make the students feel positive about band or I would not have a job next year.

"Over Thanksgiving I went home to El Paso and visited my parents. It was at this time my mother showed me your book. *(Winning Year One, A Survival Guide for First Year Teachers)*.

"I found many of the things in your book sounded exactly like me. I read it from cover to cover, twice.

"I am trying to change many of the aspects of my teaching that seem negative. I have even taken steps to be more caring and involved with the students. As a result the last two weeks have been much better. I now feel better about teaching. Class is better for the students and my personal sanity. I may even keep some of those who wanted to quit. In a nut shell, I can't thank you enough for your advice. . ."

What Happens When We Don't Give Encouragement?

When we fail to give kids what they need, when we

fail to give them encouragement and praise, we lose the war.

The language of encouragement means caring enough to give our kids the very best of ourselves.

Next we'll help save our sanity through managing kids effectively.

SUMMARY:

1. Remember the satisfied student.
2. We're into sales.
3. Have you hugged your class?
4. The avenue for praise: a footpath or freeway.
5. Give kids your best.

10 I Think As Soon As This Is Over I'll Have A Mental Meltdown

There's a mistaken belief that good teachers don't experience discipline problems. I'd like to re-phrase that—teachers who are dead have very few problems with discipline.

As long as you teach school you will encounter problems managing kids. That's the natural hazard in the job we perform. Sure, our problems won't be the first-year or second-year variety. They perhaps won't be as obvious or as easy to solve.

ONE TEACHER'S LESSON

A colleague of mine taught advanced level juniors and had one class of ninth graders, sixth hour. Mrs. Schumacher had been in the same room for twenty years. In spite of her cold demeanor with adults and young people, she cared about her students.

Yet, she deserved the button one friend of mine wore to class that read, "I have permanent PMS." The group of ninth graders gave her a great deal of trouble. Every method she had used with students in the past didn't seem to work with this group.

Their inappropriate behaviors included shouting out and refusing to do work. She began for the first time in years, sending two or three a day to the dean's office. She kept thinking that if she made it to Christmas vacation, she would be able to manage the kids better. She was wrong.

A DESPERATE SOLUTION

By late January, she had had enough. In desperation, she divided the kids into two sections—the side that would work and the side that wouldn't.

A few of the students were insulted because they did want to learn and were put on the "non-working" side.

Mrs. Schumacher ignored the "have nots," and the difficulties escalated. The non-workers chose anarchy. Soon Mrs. Schumacher was down in the principal's office rearranging five of the kids' schedules.

The "have nots" were farmed out to other classes. A few of the teachers who accepted these kids resented the imposition of taking new kids well into the second semester. It did, however, save the kids' and Mrs. Schumacher's sanity. Reports came back that the students made every effort to work for their new teachers and discipline problems didn't exist.

WHOSE FAULT IS IT ANYWAY?

Mrs. Schumacher's solution backfired. Her years of

experience were not helpful in solving this particular problem. I have some sympathy with the Mrs. Schumachers of the world, but her solution was more punishment than discipline management.

I wish I could tell you that I have never had a solution to a discipline problem backfire. Every solution won't work with every situation.

'I DON'T CARE IF THEY LIKE ME OR NOT'

When teachers say they don't wish to be liked by their students, I think they miss the entire point of student/teacher relationships. We are in a helping profession. No, kids don't have to like us every single minute of every single day. But an attitude of mutual respect or at least tolerance has to exist.

WHAT CAN 'BAD' CLASSES TEACH?

I think we all get to a point in our teaching careers when it seems we cannot learn anything new. I reached that stage after I had taught fourteen years. Then I was given a group of kids who painfully taught me to take another look.

TAKING ANOTHER LOOK

Mine was considered a "low ability level" twelfth grade English class. It should have been called a mixed ability group because the range of reading levels from non-readers to grade level was unreal. I had kids who had been mainstreamed from special education classes. One of my brightest students in the group couldn't write more than two sentences but he led class discussions with his intelligence.

I had students who drank beer before my class.

Several in the group used and sold rock cocaine.

Our school was severely overcrowded and many teachers floated. We were like transient campers. It didn't help that I used another teacher's classroom for my fourth hour group.

I shared the room with a spill over teacher. Her papers and books spilled-over onto the desk that was supposed to be mine. Student papers would mysteriously disappear. The temperature was kept at fifty degrees because that's the way the teacher who "owned the room" liked it. My students wore jeans and t-shirts and somedays shivered in the cold.

Another teacher who had taught most of these kids in previous years looked at my roll during the first day of classes and asked, "What did you do to deserve this?" I began the year with twenty-five students, twenty-four were boys.

As I got to know them better, I discovered that all but three were the youngest in their families. They were used to being the center of attention. They knew how to put adults in their service. Everyday I held my breath. Many days I wondered who was in control.

I made a great many mistakes. It is easy now to look back and analyze what I did wrong. But my major mistake was in not admitting that I had a problem. To admit that I was wrong was too threatening.

WHO CAN HELP?

I could have been helped with professional assistance. I could have invited a trusted colleague who did not know the kids to come in and observe the class.

WE'RE THE SHOW

By the end of the year, I had developed a rapport

with the group. (At that time there were only fifteen left, which helped.) I asked them why they had given me such a hard time throughout the year. Most just gave me sly little smiles. A few volunteered, "Because you were entertainment," and "Because it was fun to see you get upset."

Finding out how I had made their bad behavior pay would have been a worthwhile lesson for me to learn. But my own insecurity kept me from learning it.

OUR RELUCTANCE TO CHANGE

Could some discipline problems be the result of our reluctance to change?

In Mrs. Schumacher's situation, switching the students solved the problem for that year, but the difficulty in handling people still existed. How do you get teachers who need help coping with kids to request assistance?

The 'I Know Everything' Syndrome

It is hard for us to admit we may be wrong. The new teacher can say, "Yes, I have made some mistakes. Administrators and colleagues expect me to make mistakes." But can a fifteen-, twenty- or thirty-year veteran admit failure? Asking for help is sometimes out of the question. Why?

By the time we have been in the trenches a number of years, we develop the "I know everything" syndrome. Our pride prevents us from admitting we're wrong and asking for help. Our attitude is, "I know everything. I have seen it all. I can handle anything that comes along. I don't need deans, counselors, colleagues or principals telling me what to do with my students."

Someone once said that you should experience all

of life's problems when you are eighteen years old because that's the time when you know everything. There are lots of fifty-year-old teachers running classrooms with the same attitude.

WHAT'S THE SOLUTION?

The answer in the past has been to send teachers to staff development meetings. Teachers like Mrs. Schumacher show up with that "just try and teach me something" look. They dare a presenter to break through the indifference.

And unfortunately, some presenters are out of touch with the real world of the classroom. Or a presenter fails because he/she begins a presentation with "how to write information on a chalkboard" mentality that completely ignores the expertise found in an audience of experienced teachers.

NEEDING SOME ADJUSTMENTS DOESN'T MEAN YOU'RE MARGINAL

Just because we fail on occasion to reach one group of students, doesn't mean we have become a marginal teacher. There is a vast difference between the teacher whose expertise in working with one class falters a bit, and the teacher who can't work successfully with any students.

I don't think the term "marginal" teacher is appropriate for describing people who make mistakes. Effective teachers reach kids most of the time. Ineffective teachers fail to teach kids most of the time. There is a vast difference.

All the hundreds of thousands of dollars spent on in-service activities and hours of lecturing aren't going to improve skills that we don't possess.

If you can't reach kids, then reach out for a job you can do. Leave the schools in the hands of those who are willing to take chances, make mistakes and yes, have the courage to fail occasionally.

KNOW YOUR STRENGTHS

Know your strengths and work on the not so strong areas. Get help through college classes, books or from trusted colleagues. Try team teaching. Observe, evaluate and criticize one another.

During my fifth year of teaching I was lucky enough to be placed with an eighteen-year veteran. We team taught English and social studies. I'm sure she taught me much more than I ever taught our eighth graders.

Offer to share your area of strength in another teacher's classroom. Invite a colleague who has a particular strength into your classroom and learn from one another.

The first thing the confident, capable and caring teachers need to do is admit that *we are not perfect*. Second, recognize the areas where we are weak and do something about it.

MAKE MORE MISTAKES

Thomas Watson, the founder of IBM, said, "In order to succeed, we need to double our failure rate." Make mistakes and they will become the soil from which your success can grow.

What are your strengths? What areas need improvement? What are you doing about them?

STRIP AWAY SUPERIORITY

Perhaps it is time to strip away the mask. It is time

to say, "I don't know it all." It is O.K. to tell kids, "I am not perfect and the minute I become perfect, you will all be in big trouble. But for now, I am growing, changing and hopefully becoming a better teacher, not just for you, but for me. I hope to learn from you and I hope you will learn from me. Teach me what you know, then we will both know it."

School should be the place that when you go there, they take you in, flaws and all. And school should be the place where we are encouraged to remove the mask of superiority in reaching out to become our best selves.

Next, we will get specific about ways to share our expertise with others.

SUMMARY:

1. Veteran teachers may have discipline problems.
2. It is O.K. to ask for help.
3. Avoid the "I know everything" syndrome.
4. Know your strengths. Work to improve.
5. Remove the mask of superiority.

11 ## *Be The Public Relations Expert*

I hear often the complaint from colleagues, "Teachers just aren't professional." I think nothing could be farther from the truth.

The definition of the term, profession, is "an occupation requiring an education, especially law, medicine or teaching." Professionalism refers to our character, spirit or method of behaving as distinguished from an amateur.

Someone once said that if you wish to be rich, then you need to watch what the poor people do and don't do it.

But, if you wish to be more professional, then you need to watch what professionals do and emulate their style.

Start with your principal.

HIRE A SUCCESSFUL BOSS

Respect the person who hires you to teach. I have been lucky to have worked for principals who cared about their teachers and staffs.

If I didn't like my principal I would have fired him/ her and looked elsewhere for employment.

Because I have liked the boss, I have been willing

to carry extra responsibilities outside the teaching day. Remember the words a principal wants to hear most often are, "I'll take care of it."

My principal has been most supportive of my career. He has been a cheerleader for me, and I have been supportive of him. I will do whatever I can to help his job run smoothly.

Professionals speak well of each other. Teacher with a capital 'T'

A friend of mine is a wonderful biology instructor who loves her job. When her daughter was a high school junior, she wanted to become a teacher. Unfortunately, a counselor whom the girl adored told her she was too talented to be "just a teacher."

Her daughter is now a physical therapist and happy with her career choice. But wouldn't she have also been successful as a teacher?

When I heard this story, it reminded me of the saying from the old Pogo cartoon strip, "We have met the enemy and they are us."

If we don't speak well of our profession, then who will? The public?

Our newspapers are filled with sensational stories about schools. The really good news gets buried on page four, section E.

Is your PR showing?

Teachers complain about administrators, and administrators complain about teachers. The sad part is the public believes us both.

One busy Friday afternoon, I was waiting in the grocery store check-out line. The woman ahead of me handed the cashier a check. The cashier recognized the name on the check and said, "Oh, you're Mrs. Gibson. You teach at Orange Grove Elementary. My son goes there, and he loves it."

The exhausted teacher looked up and said, "If you worked there everyday, you'd know how bad it is."

SHOW YOUR BEST SIDE

The grocery store check-out line is not the place to air criticisms. We do our school but mostly ourselves a great disservice.

If we can't speak well of the place where we work, then we need to find a better school.

We all have bad days. Let us save our criticisms for our very close friends and intimates and show the public our best side.

WHAT YOU CONCENTRATE ON, EXPANDS

If you continually look at your teaching situation in a negative light, then you will be rewarded by having your bitterness expand.

If you try to find the good in your job and in the kids you teach, then the positive will grow. Look for things to appreciate.

ADMIRE THE TOTAL SCHOOL FAMILY

My grandmother has told me stories about fixing students' lunches and sweeping the classroom floor. If I had to fix my students' lunches, they would probably starve.

Sometimes we don't appreciate the unsung school heroes and heroines who help make our job easier.

Cafeteria Workers

Some of the kindest people I know work in school cafeterias. Could you dish up some of the meatloaf they serve and still smile?

The center of the day for most kids is lunch. A good school to the average middle schooler is one that serves french fries and chocolate shakes.

The friendly faces behind the salad bar help nourish our kids in more ways than one.

Bus Drivers

I wouldn't be a bus driver on a bet. I cannot think of a person who receives so little appreciation and who is totally responsible for the safety of our students.

Next time you see a bus driver, smile. It could be you in that blue uniform.

Custodians

Custodians are the invisible caretakers of the schools. They are invisible for one reason—their low status. No one pays any attention to them.

A newspaper article told about an elementary school cafeteria worker who was robbed in Jacksonville, Florida. A man in his mid-twenties simply took up a broom and began sweeping the sidewalk adjacent to the cafeteria.

When all the kids cleared out, he entered and held up the shocked cafeteria worker at gun point. His haul was less than $200.

After that incident, the superintendent required all personnel wear identification tags. At least in one Jacksonville elementary school, the individuals who sweep the classroom floors have an identity.

I really value the men and women who help to keep our school clean. I also believe that it is my job to pick up trash whether it is in my classroom, in the hallway or on the school's front lawn.

I have watched my principal walk the halls and pick up paper. That makes me feel that he cares. Keeping the school clean is everyone's responsibility. We are all the school's caretaker.

Secretaries

I mentioned to an assistant principal that I'd like to write a booklet for school secretaries. I'd call it, "Feel the Power."

"Please don't write that," said my friend. "They are already too powerful."

School secretaries run the schools. They are barometers for the principal. I have learned a great deal about managing people by watching our wonderful school secretaries work. They possess power. Schools can function for a day without a principal, but no school can function without secretaries.

Don't wait for secretary's week to show you care.

Librarians

The librarian is another unsung school patriot. One of my dear friends, Carol Sellers, was a teacher, a principal and then a librarian.

She is now retired on an island and spends her day collecting and categorizing shells. She told me that of all the positions she held in schools, being a librarian was her favorite. "Everyone" she told me, "loves a librarian."

PART OF A PROFESSIONAL FAMILY

Keep in mind that everyone who helps work with kids is basically trying to make this a better world. Appreciate the individual who sweeps your classroom floor and the one who smiles at you in the cafeteria line.

BREAK AWAY FROM B WING

Most of us who have been in a school a long time are isolated. We may know one wing of the school or the social studies department, well but we have no idea what goes on in the math department or even the next hallway.

Most of us are locked into our habits. We eat a tuna fish sandwich daily from the same brown paper bag. We sit with the same group of colleagues at the same cafeteria table, day in and day out. No wonder we are bored.

Try once a week to share your lunch with a different group of colleagues. Sitting with the secretaries or a group of teachers from a different subject area can add variety to the lunch experience.

Break away from B wing and see what adventures await you.

One of the best public relations tools a school system can have is a capable public speaker. Could you fit that role? We'll find out in the next chapter.

SUMMARY:

1. Hire a successful boss.
2. Be the PR expert.
3. Think teacher with a capital "T."
4. What you concentrate on, expands.
5. Appreciate the school family.
6. Break away from B wing.

12 *Giving Seminars Like A Pro*

*T*he *Book of Lists* claims that public speaking is the number one fear of Americans. Death comes in seventh with snakes and insects somewhere in between.

I'm convinced that the top leaders in any business are those individuals who have learned to share ideas well. The teacher who becomes adept at giving speeches and seminars is an asset few school systems can do without.

If we want to grow professionally, we need to be able to present information with style.

APPRECIATE YOUR EXPERTISE

What is it you do better than anyone else in your department, grade level or school? You may have organized a special reading program for first graders, or taught photosynthesis in a new and exciting way. Whatever your talent, you can turn the ideas into an effective seminar.

Make a list of ten areas where you excel as a

teacher. Narrow the list down to your top three. Talk with your colleagues and get a feel for what they would like to see presented at a conference.

REMEMBER THE 80/20 RULE

Eighty percent of the teachers will think that attending a conference is just too much trouble. But the twenty percent who do attend will be motivated. That's why sharing ideas with a convention audience is rewarding.

BUILD YOUR PROFESSIONAL IMAGE

Seminars build self-esteem. After a successful seminar, you will have a high no expensive drug can buy. Your colleagues and administrators will see you differently.

PROPER ATTIRE (WOMEN)

I saw one attractive and talented woman give a seminar in a pair of slacks. Her outfit was too casual and sexy. It detracted from what she was saying.

The best uniform is a rich-looking suit. It is better to have one good quality wool or wool blend suit than three polyester suits. Never wear pink. Follow the guidelines in the classic book by John Molloy, *The Woman's Dress For Success Book*.

He recommends grey, maroon, black or navy. I personally love red. A solid color is better than a busy print. A white blouse with navy or black projects a powerful image.

PROPER ATTIRE (MEN)

Again, I recommend John Molloy's *Dress For Success*. Another favorite book for both men and women is *The Professional Image* by Susan Bixler.

Suits for men include grey, navy, black or pin-stripped. White shirts or light blue work well, and the tie should flatter without being flashy.

Men need a great haircut that can be washed and blown dry with little effort. Socks should cover your calf, and shoes should be polished leather.

TIPS FOR SUCCESS

1. Arrive Early

Arrive forty minutes ahead of your talk. If your equipment is not set up as you had requested, it will give you time to make adjustments.

Is the temperature too hot or too cold? The temperature should be cool enough to keep everyone awake, but not too cold or too warm.

Too many chairs and empty seats in the front of the room create problems. You may want to block off the back rows with masking tape. When the room fills up, open rows as needed.

2. Write Your Introduction

There will be a person assigned to introduce you. Don't leave the introduction to chance. Write your brief introduction in about 170 words. Be honest about what you have done, giving degrees earned and awards won. Mail a copy with your acceptance letter and take a copy the day you speak.

3. The Opening

Walk toward the podium with confidence. Smile

warmly at the audience and pause. Count three seconds. Look directly at the audience and begin.

I've seen effective speakers start with a story or anecdote that ties to the theme of the seminar. Don't spend the valuable opening thanking the people who invited you. Better to begin with the theme or a powerful story that illustrates a main point.

4. Never Read Your Speech

Reading your speech marks you as an amateur, and you lose the audience. You should know your talk so well that you just about have it memorized. I said, "just about." Know your major points and be able to talk your speech with the help of a few note cards.

5. Using Note Cards

Note cards are valuable. You can add more material without having to re-type an entire seminar. They are also helpful for a quick review of your major points.

During a short seminar (forty-five minutes), I won't look through the note cards at all. During longer sessions (three hours), I give a break and will refer back to the cards to remind myself of major points.

You may want to write down key ideas on a sheet of paper and place the list on an empty chair near the center of the room.

6. Leave The Podium

Just about the worst thing you can do is stand behind the podium. Why? For one thing, the podium covers that power suit. If you are short, you look like a talking head. And you may end up clutching the sides of the podium in terror.

Walk in front of the podium and deliver your talk. If

you are using a microphone, request an extra long cord. Walk to the chair containing the highlights of your speech, and deliver your seminar.

7. *How Long Should a Seminar Be?*

Remember that the average Sunday sermon is about twenty minutes. I would rather hear a great thirty-minute talk than listen for two hours. Someone once said that a seminar is like the length of a man's swimsuit. It should be short enough to be interesting, but long enough to cover the subject.

8. *How Do You Get Over Stage Fright?*

Stage fright is the body's natural reaction to a threat. Giving seminars can be threatening. I find that stage fright is useful.

My nervousness gets my energy going. I like to hide backstage or be alone for ten minutes before facing an audience. This quiet time helps me remain calm.

I may pace, take slow deep breaths and sip warm tea. Drinking lukewarm liquids helps to relax vocal cords.

To eliminate all stage fright would be a mistake. Be alone for a few minutes, and use that energy in a positive way.

9. *Give Free Seminars*

For ten years, I volunteered to speak at state conventions for English teachers. My county paid my expenses, and I learned plenty. Speaking for free is the way to get started.

Eventually you may want to ask for an honorarium and expenses. As you gain more experience, you will feel comfortable asking for payment.

10. Write Powerful Endings

About eighty percent of your seminar will be forgotten within a few hours. What you say at the close is vital.

Give a brief summary of your main ideas. Use humor. Plan a humorous anecdote that ties in with the main theme.

Your closing should signal the end. It is the finishing touch. Make it memorable and you will be invited back to speak again.

11. Evaluations

Evaluations help us improve. Every seminar is a learning experience. Feedback in the form of magic cards or an evaluation form helps us continue to grow.

12. Write Thank You Notes

Always send thank you notes to the people who invited you. Include secretaries and others who helped to make your talk a success. The person who picks you up at the airport and makes the hotel reservation deserves this small courtesy.

THERE IS NO GUARD RAIL

I would like to end this chapter with an incident that happened to a friend of mine.

Sharon was a successful journalist who was invited to give a seminar to a group of surgeons. The information she shared was in her area of expertise; however, she regretted having accepted the invitation.

She didn't know why. She just didn't look forward to the event.

The meeting was held in a large Orlando convention hotel. She sat with ten other people, officers of the group, at a raised table with yellow linen tablecloth. She surveyed the scene—some four hundred surgeons, majority of them men, chewing stringy roast beef. Several speakers were ahead of her on the agenda and that alone made her more anxious.

Finally over apple pie she was introduced. She pushed her chair back and attempted to stand. Unfortunately, she had unknowingly pushed her chair back a tad too far.

Like being on the edge of a precipice and realizing there was no guard rail, she began an unscheduled descent.

She grabbed the air, then reached a steel grip on the edge of the tablecloth. You have seen those magicians who can pull out a tablecloth and leave all the contents of a full course dinner nicely in place. Unfortunately my friend had no magical powers that evening.

The cloth kept her from falling backwards but peas, gravy, mashed potatoes and apple pie were momentarily airborne, then deposited back on the table in a new and crazy design.

With the grace of a dancer, she wrapped the tablecloth around herself like a shawl and headed for the microphone. She said in a deep, sultry voice, "And you thought there wouldn't be any entertainment."

Having style in the face of disaster, making the most of a moment no matter how ludicrous that moment may be, are the necessary skills for giving successful seminars.

If you can learn to expect the unpredictable you will learn plenty from every disaster.

It can be frightening to speak before your colleagues. Put your fears aside. Be brave. Take the risk. Give seminars. It will do wonders for your self-confidence and for your career. Good luck in your public speaking adventures.

Next, we will polish our professional image.

SUMMARY:

1. Appreciate your expertise—speak!
2. Look professional.
3. Step in front of the podium.
4. Arrive early. Set the stage.
5. Prepare your own introduction.
6. Expect the unpredictable.

13 *How Clothes Create Our Professional Image*

When we are meeting people for the first time, we are judged within six seconds by the way we are dressed.

Jim and Tammy Faye Bakker were caught embezzling thousands of dollars from the ministry they established. A well known media advisor, Dorothy Samoff, felt their attire should have warned us.

"Sometimes I think Jim Bakker had too many buttons opened. He had too much hair showing on his chest. Tammy Faye wore false eyelashes and heavy make-up. Her bosoms featured to the camera were theatrical rather than religious."

We are more comfortable when people dress for the part. When our credibility is in question, we need to wear a power suit. That's exactly what Oliver North did.

ESTABLISHING CREDIBILITY

Oliver North was accused and later found guilty of helping finance illegal military operations in Nicaragua.

When his hearings were held on national television, he dressed in a crisp Marine uniform. His pressed shirt and straightened tie all established believability.

Clothes serve us

Our attire should serve our purposes, not the other way around. Sales personnel in expensive department stores follow dress codes. Managers know that the sales clerk must dress to make the sale.

Have you ever visited the cosmetic counter in a large department store and seen a poorly made-up sales woman? No. The woman behind the cosmetic counter has a flawlessly made up face. She is trying to make the sale.

In addition, the cosmetic sales person wears a white smock which adds another professional touch. She looks beautiful and authoritative. How can we resist the expensive lipstick?

What is your professional image?

There are many ways to look professional and well dressed. I am not about to tell you what to wear in your classroom.

I happen to prefer suits. I like them for many reasons. One, they are easy to wear. I leave my house at six-thirty in the morning, and anything that quickens my departure from home is helpful.

Suits and blazers and skirts are flattering. They give me a boost of confidence. Professional people in positions of power and respect wear the uniform of the professional—the suit.

WHAT IS YOUR SUPERINTENDENT WEARING TODAY?

Someone once said that we should dress for the position we hope to have one day. Does your superintendent wear a suit? What about your principal?

WEAR WHAT IS APPROPRIATE

On her campaign trail, I was able to meet a woman who later became education commissioner for the state of Florida. Like most professionals, she wore a suit.

While visiting elementary schools, she soon learned that the suit made her less approachable. The young children were accustomed to seeing their teachers in dresses. On the mornings she visited elementary schools, she wore a dress and left her jacket in the car.

She adjusted her attire to match the needs of her audience. Did it make a difference? Well, she was elected.

WHAT ISN'T APPROPRIATE

I don't feel that jeans are appropriate. There's one very good reason. Jeans are the uniform of the young. Sure many adults wear jeans. They are comfortable. I love them for weekends.

DOWDY ISN'T IN

A dear friend of mine went through the typical mid-life crisis. It began when she was about forty.

She moved to Florida from Indiana and continued her teaching career at my school.

Her clothes could be described in one word: dowdy. Although she had a good figure, it was buried by baggy slacks and loose tops. She had beautiful skin and eyes but wore little make-up.

She was, however, an excellent teacher. Her turning point came when she was sent to a major university for a three-week intensive teacher training session. She came back with confidence and energy I had never seen.

Before the school year began, she had a complete make-over. She went to a clothing and make-up consultant who gave her a new look. She had her hair frosted. She began an exercise program.

Bolstered by her new look, she applied for and landed a job in a newly opened high school. That was two years ago. Her principal has given her lots of responsibility and recognition.

She is now about forty-five, still well-loved by her students and at the top of her profession. This summer she will be leading a training session in England.

Would she have been as successful in her former attire? I don't think so. The changes in her appearance were part of the changes in her attitude and outlook on life. It was all part of her professionalism.

LOOKING GOOD
DOESN'T HAVE TO COST A FORTUNE

Looking well-dressed does not mean paying large sums of money. I buy most of my suits on sale or at discount stores. Buy quality items. Select classic lines and colors that flatter.

Our clothes should fit our personalities and our teaching situations. They should "sell" us and make us feel good about ourselves. They should have pizzazz because, after all, we are professional teachers.

What else creates the professional?

Business Cards

About ten years ago, I started doing workshops in creative writing. One seminar was called, "I Hate Poetry." I was invited to speak at a state convention of English teachers. Later, school systems in Florida became interested in my talk.

I felt that a business card would be an asset, so I went to a printer and for a small price had some cards made. When did I use them? At state and national conventions. Handing over my card during introductions helped people remember me.

The administrators in your school system most likely have business cards. Why not you?

Stationery

About the same time I printed business cards, I had my first stationery printed. I have placed copies of the stationery and business cards in the appendix at the back of the book.

I use the stationery when writing letters to parents and administrators. It is also helpful when applying for county or state grants. My own letterhead is another link in the professional chain.

Professional Organizations

Become involved in your professional organization on the local, state and national level. Offer to teach a workshop or hold an office. You will meet like-minded individuals and gain new skills.

Apply to attend state and national conventions. It has been estimated that only twenty percent of the teachers attend their conventions. Be part of that select group.

Convention tips

Conventions are great places to meet people. For your own sanity, leave your family at home. Be friendly. Introduce yourself.

If you go with a group, break away from them. Perhaps meet for dinner but try to attend different sessions so you will have information to share when you get back together.

Wear your name tag on your right shoulder. Why? Because when you shake hands, your name will be visible and easier to read. Wear your friendliest face. Go and expect to make new friends.

Society expects more from us than from most professionals

Did you read about Charles Koopman? He was the high school social science teacher who was given fifty years in prison. What was the crime? He mailed cocaine from Bolivia to an ex-student in Tampa, Florida.

The twenty-nine-year-old teacher mailed the cocaine to a seventeen-year-old student. In sentencing him, the judge admonished him for the crime. He said, "You are a teacher in a position of authority and influence. If I don't send you to jail, who am I going to put in jail for delivering cocaine?"

I think what was so shocking about this drug case was that a teacher was involved. A real estate agent or a used car salesperson might have been given a lesser sentence.

We are held in high esteem by the community. We are respected by other professions. Let's look and act the part.

SUMMARY:

1. Dress like the professional.
2. Support your principal.
3. Use business cards and stationery.
4. Join professional organizations.
5. Attend conventions.
6. Know that you are respected.

14 Adults Only: The Intimate Place No One Can Touch

My friend Bill and I were invited to a neighbor's house for his surprise birthday supper. The neighbors had invited twenty of Bill's friends. The dinner was complete with birthday cake and many brilliant candles. However, when Bill attempted to blow out the candles he soon realized it was impossible. Trick party candles were used. The moment they appeared to be blown out, they came right back.

Long-term teachers in classrooms across this country are expected to have all the characteristics of a trick party candle. We are expected to keep coming back.

Our energy and enthusiasm is the fuel that lights our motivation. Before I can motivate kids, I need to feel motivated myself. Throughout the school year, my energy has high and low periods. How do I pull myself through a slump? That's what we'll discuss in this chapter.

LIGHT YOUR ENTHUSIASM

1. Create Change

An experiment with a group of General Electric workers showed the power that change had on the workplace. The interesting facet of the Hawthorn Effect, as this experiment was called, was that minor changes in the physical environment improved productivity.

For example, when the lights in a factory were lowered, productivity increased. When the lights were made brighter, productivity also increased. The stimulation brought about by change was the key.

Physical changes in our classrooms can include rearranging the room, decorating the walls with student art/writing, playing classical music before class starts, etc. Any small break from the routine will be a welcomed relief. The change doesn't have to be major to be effective.

ENLIVEN YOUR OUTLOOK: SWITCH CLASSES

Two friends of mine who teach near Denver did a week-long experiment. They both taught science, one on the high school and the other on the middle school level. They decided to switch classes for a week.

The high school teacher was amazed at the amount of time spent on discipline at the middle school level. The middle school teacher was appalled by the apathy found with some high school students.

They both felt the project made them appreciate their own level of teaching. It was such a success that the next year they extended the time to two weeks.

If you want to try this experiment, start with your own school. Switch with a colleague and teach for a thirty-minute period. You will be amazed at what the change will teach.

The stimulation of change, whether it's a minor

112

physical adjustment or a major class switch, will add zest and excitement.

2. Remember To Laugh

In Norman Cousin's book *Anatomy of an Illness,* he describes how watching *Candid Camera* and other humorous television shows helped him overcome a near-fatal disease.

Bernie Siegel, M.D., has written extensively on the power of our minds to help us with disease.

A good belly laugh is healing. A friend I teach with collects corny jokes and silly puns. I try to see him once a day just for the quick fix—the laugh. It helps lift my spirits.

A DAILY DOSE OF LAUGHTER

If we can't fall down laughing hysterically at least once a day at the absurdities that go on within classroom walls, at bus stops and in the hallways of our schools, then we are living in another solar system.

Ridiculousness is out there. Not seeing it is our mistake. Trust your sense of humor to keep you sane.

According to one comedian, laughter is like changing a baby's wet diaper. It doesn't change anything permanently but it sure makes us feel better for awhile.

3. Tell Your Face

The first grader came bouncing into the classroom. She noticed the teacher's frown and asked what was wrong. The teacher's gruff, "Nothing's wrong," didn't satisfy the child. She looked up and asked, "Then why don't you tell your face."

Smiling does make us feel better. Our brain picks up cues from our facial expression. It is impossible for us to hold two emotions simultaneously. When you are in a good mood, try frowning into a mirror. You will soon start to laugh because holding those two opposing emotions is impossible.

If I weren't happy and smiling in the classroom, then I couldn't teach. My facial expression reflects my attitude. Have you noticed colleagues and perhaps administrators who appear to have their smiles surgically removed? What statement does that make to kids?

As a beginning teacher, I often heard the warning, "Don't smile until Christmas." However, the research is contrary to that old adage.

It might be difficult to smile when you don't feel like it, but it's a lot tougher to face a colleague or teacher whose only expression is a sneer or grimace.

4. Our Internal Voice

It has been estimated that we keep an internal conversation going at the rate of eight hundred to one thousand words per minute. We create a climate with our inner talk that makes us happy or sad, strong or weak.

Our day doesn't begin with the ringing of an alarm clock. It begins with our reaction to that dark morning bell. We can begin the day with, "Oh, God, it's morning," or "Thank, God, lovely morning." The choice is up to us.

5. Mini-Vacations

Many school systems throughout the country give teachers a half-year or full year sabbatical for worthwhile projects like attaining advanced degrees, writing books, or traveling extensively. A few months or full year can do wonders to increase energy and enthusiasm.

But not all of us can afford the time away from family and other commitments. That's where the shorter, mini-vacation comes in.

State and national conventions are held in late October and November. They usually include a weekend and are wonderful ways not only to get a break from home obligations, but ways to regain enthusiasm. Most of the very best presenters are teachers who have used new methods with their kids and are eager to share ideas.

Our mini-vacation doesn't have to take us far from home. I sometimes pack a picnic supper and head for an island just north of Sanibel. A few hours on the beach is almost as good as a weekend away without the expense.

Attend conventions and take short mini-vacations to help restore your energy. The rewards will be great.

6. Feeding Inspiration

We spend a great deal of time and money on our physical life, but what about our spiritual well being? A good teacher is like a faith-healer. We sometimes see possibilities where no one else does.

Who inspires and nurtures the teacher?

We need an inspirational source that can include colleagues, mentors, books and cassettes.

Replenishing our supply of inspiration is a great investment in our mental and spiritual selves.

7. Personal Inventory Checklist

Kids are great readers of adult body language. They may not always interpret the signals correctly, but they are very much aware of our facial expressions, our posture and our movements. The following checklist will help you analyze your own body language.

What is my facial expression as I:
enter the building?

greet colleagues?
greet students?

What is my posture as I:
    walk from the parking lot into the school?
    walk down the hallway and enter the office?
    stand before my students in the morning?

Do I recognize and speak to:
    custodians, bus drivers, cafeteria workers,
    secretaries, aides, etc.?

Do I make eye contact?

Do I call colleagues and students by name?

What about my voice?
    Am I loud enough to be heard easily?
    Is my voice strong, confident and cheerful?

SPIRITUAL HEALTH

A columnist for our local paper writes about physical well being. One article began with the statement: "If you don't take care of your body where will you live?"

The same is true about our spiritual selves. If we don't take care of our inspirational sources, then where will our soul live?

What have you done for your spiritual self lately?

BLAZING CANDLES

We would all like to keep the candle of our inspiration and enthusiasm burning brightly. In this chapter I have not mentioned one of the richest sources for encouragement—the kids themselves.

Encouragement comes when we see that grin of recognition when a student says, "Yes, I understand." It is wonderful when kids say, "That was easy," about a newly learned skill.

It is also encouraging to have "kids" now grown come back to say, "Hello," and, "Thank you for helping me."

Of all the emotions, the most difficult to keep for long is gratitude. Perhaps that is why I waited until the end of this chapter to mention gratitude as a source of encouragement.

I ran into a former student in the mall. It had been three years since she had graduated. She was so beautiful and mature looking that I hardly recognized her. She looked me directly in my eyes and said, "I meant to thank you when I was still in school . . . I'm glad I have the chance to do this now . . . thank you for being a good teacher."

I don't think that I did anything special for this young woman. I just did the best I could and maybe for her that was enough.

Even though gratitude might be expressed briefly, let's recognize it through the smile of recognition, through interest or enthusiasm and through a touch. Find ways to appreciate the "thank you" when kids say it.

If the teacher's enthusiasm is supposed to be like a trick party candle then we had better find a way to keep the light of enthusiasm burning brightly.

Keep inspired for yourself. Seek and find your spiritual source. You deserve it. And so do your kids.

SUMMARY:

1. Use change to light your enthusiasm.
2. Find a laugh a day.
3. Tell your face to be happy.
4. Feed your inspirational side.
5. Recognize appreciation in a smile or a touch.

15 *Cooperative Teaching*

I grew up in Miami, Florida, and learned how to sail on Biscayne Bay. Racing the small, optimist pram was more than just a sport. It was my initiation into the world of competition and cooperation.

Every Saturday and Sunday I spent with my three brothers and at least thirty other kids aged nine to fourteen, learning the finer techniques of sailing. I sharpened my people skills in the process.

When the races began, I knew exactly who my competition was and I had learned a strategy for trying to outwit them. It was friendly competition at its finest.

When the races were over, we headed our small crafts into shore. We all pitched in to haul boats, wash sails and load the prams until another weekend.

We laughed a great deal, sometimes fought but always knew the value of team work and the value of helping one another.

I credit my parents for introducing me to this wonderful exciting world of cooperation and competition.

I see kids in classrooms across this country who do not understand the skills necessary for cooperation.

Perhaps they haven't been taught by their parents. Perhaps they haven't had the opportunity of team sports or sailboat races.

MY OBLIGATION AS TEACHER

Course content and skills are necessary and required by law to be taught, but the skills of cooperation and compromise are just as vital and necessary as the curriculum guide.

When students leave my classroom in June, I want them to know one another very well and to feel a closeness for one another.

END-OF-THE-YEAR COMMENTS

When students write end-of-the-year comments, it helps me learn if my attempts have been successful. The following statements are unedited samplings of their remarks:

"I didn't believe you when you gave us that speech in the beginning of the year about 'growing closer together,' but I've gotten to know more people in this class than any other. I think all the group activities we do is the cause."

"This was a class filled with friendly people. I got to know many students in this class because everybody helped each other out."

"Getting to know people is something I'm good at. And in this class I was able to make 20 more friends. Also when I know people it's easier for me to get involved. I'm glad my senior year turned out as good as I expected."

"Some of the things I liked about the course was the way the students got along. Everybody knew and liked each other and there was never any trouble.

Although it was a lot of work, I learned a lot. It was easy for people to express their opinions in a group."

I was pleased that my students felt a closeness and I credit cooperative teaching for that success.

COOPERATIVE TEACHING DEFINED

I am sure that as an experienced educator, you have read books and attended seminars on cooperative learning.

Cooperative teaching is a method of instruction that gets kids working together. Cooperative learning takes place when kids have been able to get to know one another. Teaching social skills becomes a part of teaching content.

COOPERATIVE TEACHING
IS JUST ONE ALTERNATIVE

Cooperative teaching should not exclude all other techniques for reaching kids. There is solid research behind this method, and it's a technique that works well.

Robert Slavin from John Hopkins University suggests that the process of learning cooperatively improves retention of skills and content. When kids are forced to explain ideas to one another, they process the information in a new way.

Teaching someone else sets up a powerful learning experience. However, cooperative learning in itself doesn't answer all our problems.

I still believe that the best approach to helping kids is not one approach, but a combination of group work, individual work, lecture, etc. An eclectic approach to teaching works best.

TEACHING THE SKILLS OF COOPERATION

In order for kids to work together, they need to be

aware of the social skills necessary for cooperation. When they leave our classroom and have questions in the work place, they will go to friends and fellow employees for the answers. They most likely won't ask the boss.

Teams write reports and solve problems so learning how to be a team player is vital.

THE IMPORTANCE OF EYE CONTACT

I see former students quite frequently. I usually ask them, "What did you learn in my class that has helped you now that you're out of school?"

I am always hoping that something they learned in English literature will be beneficial to them later. I was in a store buying shoes when I heard a familiar sounding voice.

Sandy was in her second year of college, working as a sales clerk for the summer. She said what helped her the most was the fact that she had to give speeches in my class and that she learned to give eye contact.

"Giving eye contact has helped me sell more shoes."

Unfortunately, unless they have had a speech course, most students, even high school seniors, don't know about making eye contact.

Dustin Hoffman, while doing the movie *Rain Man*, said that his toughest job was not the realistic portrayal of an autistic man. His most difficult task was that when he spoke to

Tom Cruise, he couldn't give any eye contact.

Many of our kids are not accustomed to giving eye contact to friends, family or teachers. It has been estimated that most teenagers spend less than thirty minutes a week of quality time with parents.

No wonder kids have difficulty communicating in groups. One way to teach eye contact is to demand it when talking with kids. Expressions like, "Give me your eyes," and "Eyes on me," work well.

Frequent monitoring of the groups and group evaluations with eye contact required are just two ways to make sure your cooperative teams are using this valuable skill.

TEACHING ACTIVE LISTENING

Students can learn to use phrases which will help clarify ideas. Terms like:

"I think what you are saying is . . ."
"I think I understand you to mean . . ."

help us to hear the idea in another form. Active listening goes along with proper body language.

TEACHING BODY LANGUAGE

At the beginning of the year, teach kids about the importance of body language. I usually explain it this way:

"Try and imagine an invisible bubble around you, that measures approximately twelve inches around your body. This is your personal, private space. The only people we allow to invade our bubble are close family members, such as boyfriend/girlfriend, mother/father, etc.

"Sometimes people invade our space with a fist, and that makes us want to fight back. Others invade our space with a kiss, and sometimes that makes us want to run or get closer, depending on our feelings.

"There are differences in the way people from other countries handle this bubble. I have a neighbor from Austria. I usually see him at neighborhood parties, and he stands very close to me. I have a tendency to step back a little because he is inside my comfort zone. For him, however, the distance is just fine, and he sometimes steps a little closer because too much distance makes him uncomfortable.

"An elevator is the perfect example of a place where standing close to strangers is acceptable. When you work in groups of two or three, it is necessary to sit close enough so that a soft voice can be used and still be heard."

I think the most crucial part of this talk on body language is my demonstration of how kids cooperate or fail to cooperate in groups. First, I role play the part of a reluctant student.

I demonstrate the body language and attitude of an individual who hates getting into groups.

"Oh, I can't sit next to Roger. He hasn't had his shots this month. Why do we have to do this stupid stuff anyway? I just hate this."

Then, I demonstrate a student who is willing to work on a team.

My students' usual response is laughter, but they clearly get the message.

MONITORING THE GROUPS

We all have a tendency to perform better when we are being observed. I do my best sit-ups when the aerobics instructor leaves the front of the class and announces that he will be checking our form.

Visiting with all the groups is vital. Sitting with our

teams, listening and making notes are just some of the ways to monitor the groups.

SELF-MONITORING

The groups need to be monitored by the teacher, but they also should be self-monitoring. Ask students to name three positive body language responses seen in group members. This will help focus on the positive.

BEHAVIORS THAT SHOW DISINTEREST

Have students write and share with the class a list of behaviors that show disinterest. These might include: arms folded across chest, legs crossed, leaning back in chair, eyes to ceiling and a physical distance from the group.

Another effective and popular behavior that shows indifference is the student who builds a wall of books and occasionally peers from behind the stack. A distance of more than a foot between chairs or desks will further isolate group members.

TEACHING KIDS TO SHARE THE WORK

We discuss the definition of a free loader. Because Florida has mild winters, most of my students are familiar with the relative who shows up in February with a t-shirt and ten dollar bill and doesn't change either for a month.

I also point out that sometimes we get a house guest who perhaps shares your home but in exchange allows you to drive his new red Ferrari to school.

I tell students to do their fair share because they are no longer working for me alone, but for themselves and for the good of the group.

SETTING A TIME LIMIT

Most of us give too much time for group activities.

Giving too much time is much worse than giving too little time.

A shorter time frame establishes urgency. It helps kids learn to work smarter rather than just working harder. We all have seen classrooms where kids are given thirty minutes to complete ten minutes of work. Kids will discuss last week's party, then rush through the assignment in the remaining minutes.

SETTING UP YOUR GROUPS

The teams can be as varied as the activities. I generally set up permanent groups for a nine-week period. These are three-person teams. I also like to form groups of kids with six or seven per team, so I sometimes combine groups.

ARE YOU A NEWCOMER?

You might wish to observe another teacher's class who uses cooperative teaching techniques. There are plenty of books and workshops on the subject.

For the newcomer, the smaller two-person teams or three-person teams work best.

ADVANTAGES OF COOPERATIVE TEACHING

We have already seen that working in teams helps create close friendships. Kids also learn to listen better, to appreciate others and to share leadership as well as responsibility.

EVERYONE SITS IN THE BIG CHAIR

The biggest advantage of all for using cooperative teaching techniques is that all the kids get to be stars.

They all sit at the big desk.

I have a rocking chair at the back of my classroom. It is bright purple, one of the school's colors. During an open house, I had a parent come for a brief visit with his five-year-old daughter.

While Dad and I were talking, the little girl crawled up into the rocking chair. Her father noticed her and said, "Don't sit in the big chair. That's for the teacher."

I told the father that his daughter was fine. It wasn't my chair, but the class' chair. Everyone used it.

That is what makes cooperative teaching so much fun. Everyone gets a chance to teach. The focus is not on the teacher, but on the student.

I AM THE ROLE MODEL

I am the role model for cooperation. My behavior toward my principal, school secretary, counselor, deans, colleagues and custodians is carefully observed by my kids. My ability to get along with the school team is the subject for the next chapter.

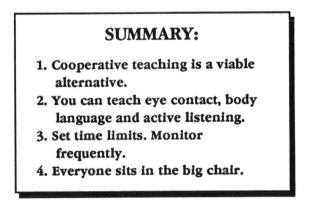

SUMMARY:

1. Cooperative teaching is a viable alternative.
2. You can teach eye contact, body language and active listening.
3. Set time limits. Monitor frequently.
4. Everyone sits in the big chair.

16 Sex, Lies And When Ted Met Alice—How To Stay Healthy And Happy Without Going Insane

The experts agree that if we wish to be healthy, then we need to be content and happy in two areas: our homes and our professions.

I work with colleagues whose home lives are in shambles. Their one area of success is the classroom. Maintaining a balanced marriage or sustaining a permanent relationship seems almost impossible.

A balanced life is a healthy life. Robert Fulghum, in his charming book *All I Really Needed To Know I Learned In Kindergarten,* advises that we, "draw, paint, sing and dance, play and work every day."

Some of us live lives that are 75 percent teaching and 25 percent drudgery. We forget the wisdom of playing, singing, dancing and even talking and listening to one another.

LIVES THAT ARE ASKEW

When we create lives that are askew, we live lives without harmony. We sometimes help to make ourselves ill.

I know. I have had cancer. A life-threatening disease does one thing quite well. It helps you focus on what is most important.

One of my best friends, a writer, lost his life to lung cancer when he was thirty-eight years old. Jim McLendon was a college buddy who wrote me a letter about two months before he died.

Ironically, at the time he felt that he was regaining his health. His letter said something I will never forget. "You make yourself sick and you make yourself well."

When I looked back over the year or two preceding my cancer, I realized I had a part in the disease. I was working long hours. I took little time off to unwind and really relax. Because most of my energies were invested in my work, my relationship with my husband was not the best it could be.

I really believe that I contributed to my disease. I now contribute to my wellness. My life is in harmony. I do something pleasurable everyday. If something pleasurable hasn't happened by four o'clock, I make it happen.

MARRIAGE IN REVIEW

I have spent the last 127 pages giving you tips, suggestions and ideas for improving your work as a teacher.

All my advice about classroom management and motivation will fail if you don't have a strong sense of yourself. Even when you try to implement these ideas, they will fail if your personal life is shambles. What happens outside the classroom walls has a tremendous effect on your ability to relate and teach children.

Although I have been successful within the classroom my personal life has not been easy. This book would be incomplete without my acknowledging my own personal struggles in my marriage and divorce.

We met and married in college. Although my husband and I never had children, I always felt the children in my classroom were my own. We were married 22 years.

During the last year of my marriage, my forty-something husband had an extended affair. I knew the marriage was in deep trouble but I did one thing most caregivers do, I blamed myself.

I mistakenly thought that I could fix what was wrong. I felt I had concentrated too much energy on my books and seminars. I decided to be a better wife. I cooked gourmet dinners, worked out and kept the house clean. My efforts failed.

I felt more and more distance between us and looked forward to business trips out of town. I dreaded returning home.

Finally on New Year's Eve, my husband honestly answered my questions. He told me he was in love with someone else. Then he moved out. I was stunned. I had a difficult time accepting reality.

CHANGE AS THE TEACHER

Change can be a tremendous teacher, but most of us don't welcome change. Remember in *Wayne's World* when Benjamin suggested a change in the show and Garth said, "We fear change." Then he started pounding on a mechanical hand with that deranged look on his face?

Just like Garth, it took some time for me to accept the upheaval in my life. I recall sitting in a rocking chair for hours, thinking to myself, what will happen to me? Having moved from a college dorm to married life, I had never lived alone. The impending change terrified me.

I had to make a choice. Do I continue hoping,

praying and wishing that the man I loved would return home? Or do I pick up the pieces as best I can, and go forward with my life?

SHIFTING GEARS

I decided I could be successful without a husband. Three months after the breakup, I was divorced on my birthday. It was terribly sad, but a part of me felt reborn. I began a new life.

How does this relate to teaching? I learned many valuable lessons from the divorce. The key lesson I learned was that we need to live in reality. We need to see our lives as they really are and not as we wish them to be.

We also need to be clear on the fact that everything that happens in our personal lives effects our teaching. Just as what occurs in the classroom colors our emotional worlds, what occurs at home impacts our teaching.

LIVING THE UNBALANCED LIFE

When relationships fail, we don't always live a balanced life. One high school teacher expressed it this way, "My relationship with a husband was not giving me what I needed. I found success at school. The more committees I ran, the more my colleagues and my principal expected of me. I was called upon because I could get things done. I realize now I volunteered to spend extra time with the kids because they helped me avoid going home. When I went home my husband complained that he didn't see enough of me. No one complained at school. They loved me at school. From the principal's point of view I must have been his best employee. I needed to get a better sense of what I was doing. You should tell teachers that when they find themselves in this role, that something is askew in their lives. They need to take the time to find out what that something is."

Even the best teachers face adversity and crisis. Life is a struggle. Bad things happen to good teachers all the time. Ironically my own problems helped me relate better to adults and to students experiencing the same struggles.

I have had teachers tell me after a seminar that they had heard me several years before my marriage failed, and that I'm a better speaker now.

OUR BEST LESSONS

Our best lessons may not come from our students, colleagues or classrooms. Our best lessons may come from life itself. We need to pay close attention to the quality of our lives. We need to look at our relationships and ask how they can be improved. We need to talk about what we want and need with the people we share our lives. We need to build friendships and not expect one teaching job and one relationship to fill all our needs.

LISTEN TO OUR SUBCONSCIOUS

We need to pay attention to ourselves and to our subconscious. Our subconscious mind sends us valuable information. We only need to listen. During the year my marriage was failing, I sensed my husband was involved with someone else but my irrational thinking was, "He would never cheat on me." So I dismissed those strong emotional feelings. That was a mistake.

Someone once said what doesn't kill you, makes you stronger. I feel stronger than ever. Overcoming adversity destroys us or make us a hero. When a personal crisis occurs, we need to be brave and face reality. When our personal life is together, we have a much better chance of being the teacher kids need to have.

If we take the time to pay attention to our feelings, they will tell us the truth. We need to trust our intuition and subconscious because they teach us lessons we can't learn in school.

When is your time together?

Set aside at least ten minutes per day to express feelings. Just giving a running account of "guess what happened to me today" is not the same thing as talking about how you felt about what occurred.

One of my friends is an expert on marriage, having been married three times. When she was with her first husband, Susan fell in love with her gynecologist. She saw him as a "knight in sparkling stethoscope."

She soon discovered that the knight was a workaholic. After several years she convinced him to add another doctor to his busy practice. She confided in me that she realized the marriage was over when he still left the house at six a.m., although he had hired extra staff to carry the work load.

His career came before her. Perhaps if they had created a little time for one another every day, they would still be married.

Did you get a happiness example?

They say that if you want a good marriage, pick

132

parents who are/were happily married. Unfortunately that is about as likely as winning at the lottery.

The solution is to find a current happiness model. I like socializing with other couples who are happy. Their love spills over onto me. So if you couldn't pick happy parents, pick happy friends.

Another friend of mine relates that when she was a little girl, she remembers waking up in the night and hearing her parents talking in bed. She says that now as an adult, that is one of her fondest memories. When we really communicate with one another, we give a gift to ourselves as well as our children .

THE MUTUAL PAIN OF PMS

In the film *Steel Magnolias,* one of the actresses says, "I don't have PMS. I've just been in a very bad mood for the last thirty-six years."

There are many jokes around about the phenomena known as pre-menstrual syndrome.

Research indicates that more crimes by women are committed in the days prior to menstruation. More than half of the women who attempt suicide, do so in the few days prior to the onset of their period. For some women the cyclic changes of estrogen and progesterone may bring about immense or infinitesimal changes. It varies greatly.

What does this have to do with teaching? If we mark our calendars, we may be able to understand our mood swings and try to avoid confrontations with kids on the day or two before our period.

A little sensitivity from our male colleagues, husbands or boyfriends is also in order. A wonderful couple I know has developed a great way of dealing with this very real problem. When Sandy becomes highly emotional or unusually aggressive, Dave, her husband, says to her, "Honey, let's check the calendar." Nine times out of ten, Sally has admitted that her violent mood swings can be attributed to PMS.

The funny part is that when she recognizes the problems, she immediately calms down. "I realize", she tells me, "that I am not losing my mind after all."

Along with a little sensitivity, what else can we do to maintain loving relationships?

LAUGH TOGETHER DAILY

Laughing together each day is one of the best ways to maintain our perspective. Save one funny story to share with the one you love. Teaching gives us lots of stories to share.

One colleague introduces her husband at parties with the words, "He's my first husband." She explains that it keeps him alert.

THE UNIVERSE'S BELL SCHEDULE

I believe that the universe has a bell schedule. Many times we refuse to hear the warning bells, and we get into trouble.

Sometimes when the universe's bell rings, we see it as a major inconvenience in our personal agenda.

One early morning, I was on a tight schedule, flying to Washington state to give a keynote address. I was sitting in the plane, listening to the flight attendants, and wondering what was for breakfast.

The pilot interrupted the flight attendants' safety spiel with the announcement that a major engine part was malfunctioning and that we would have to leave the plane, get re-ticketed and re-board four hours later.

We were not happy fliers. We jumped up and

134

immediately started complaining about our missed meetings and broken connections.

On my way down the aisle, an older attractive lady said that we should be grateful that the pilot noticed the malfunctioning part in enough time to delay take-off. The universe's bell schedule? I believe so.

I did arrive in Washington many hours later and received a $150 voucher toward my next plane ticket. Life does unfold as it should. We are all children listening to the universe's clock.

What we all need to learn is to become happier fliers.

Try to find satisfaction at school and at home, and you will rarely visit the doctor's office. Share with your loved ones your real feelings. Allow time each day for laughing and playing. Remember to listen for the universe's bell schedule.

SUMMARY:

1. Live a balanced life.
2. Take time to listen and to talk.
3. Our best lessons come through life itself.
4. Get on the universe's bell schedule.

17 *Is This All There Is?*
Is This All I've Got?

My friend and I attended a popular play in a large theatre. It was two and one half hours until the much needed intermission. The line to the ladies' room wound around the lobby.

We were on a university campus. I left the line and found a deserted restroom in the next building. In less than five minutes, I returned to the long line to let the other women know about this wonderful convenience.

I was giving simple directions to one lady at the back of the line, when the woman in front of her turned around and said, "I don't know. Are we allowed?"

ARE YOU WAITING IN LINE

Too many of us are waiting in line, hoping that someone will come along and grant us permission to do the things in our lives we most want to do.

We have been told:

> *"Don't fight the system."*
> *"Don't break the rules."*

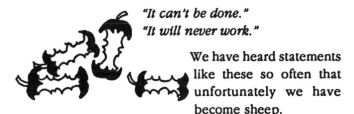

"It can't be done."
"It will never work."

We have heard statements like these so often that unfortunately we have become sheep.

We don't need parental permission or approval anymore. Now is the time to find our lives exciting and satisfying. Grant yourself permission to change the things you can no longer tolerate.

Jimmy Buffet said in a song, "I'd rather die when I'm living than live while I'm dead."

The problem is that some teachers throughout this country are in classrooms where they are dying.

Brave, courageous, risk-taking teachers exit when they feel the time is right. Weak, unhappy and passive teachers stay because they fear their own potential. They lack the courage to act.

DON'T KILL THE KIDS

The trouble with staying when we would rather go is that in the process of denying ourselves real power, we destroy our students. They suffer.

THE RED PEN WEAPON

Students' grades become the ultimate weapon. The power of the red pen rules the world. I have heard teachers say, "I grade a paper until it's bloody." I've seen those papers.

The kid gets his paper back and he can't read it. He has nothing left. There is no desire to try again. He is stripped of self-esteem.

That is not teaching. That is crucifixion. Getting

kids to be successful doesn't mean killing their energy, enthusiasm and confidence.

Schools need encouragers not executioners. Kids need teachers who care and who listen, not flawless, omnipotent rulers.

BUT WHAT ABOUT THE CONTRADICTION?

One teacher expressed it this way: "I don't have time to value myself." Then make time.

Before we can value students, we first need to value ourselves. If we cannot appreciate ourselves and our profession, then no one else will be able to.

Gather people around you who support you and your good teaching. If your significant other doesn't like your career and you do, it is time to trade up.

One teacher wrote on an evaluation at the close of a workshop that, "My boyfriend wished I wouldn't enjoy teaching so much." Time to change boyfriends.

Another man wrote, "My wife is very supportive. She thinks I can do it all." Grab hold of this valuable woman.

The people we eat breakfast with should be there to support our decision to leave or to stay.

If we decide to leave, then we need to do something today to help us reach our goals.

Stop reading this book and start typing your resume. Call about taking a personal or professional leave. Do something constructive to make your goal a reality.

AND IF WE STAY . . .

And if we decide to stay, walk into the classroom like a prize fighter before a big match. Be confident and cocky. Show your good face. Expect to win.

In a sense, we are all prize fighters. Fighting for what we believe is right for our own personal happiness, our sanity and our survival. Good luck, prize fighter.

138

18 *When Do I Graduate?*

hen I went in for a minor biopsy, I thought I had a problem. When the doctor came out and said, "breast cancer" I knew I faced the biggest opportunity of my life.

Three weeks after surgery, I was scheduled to give a time management seminar for teachers. My friends said, "Cancel." I said that I had to go. It was my coming out party, the debutante's dance of survival and life. I couldn't miss it.

A blonde angel disguised as a middle school English teacher drove my Ford Bronco the four hours to Tampa for the convention. Her name was Vicki Stockman. She was my roommate, car mate and laugh mate.

She helped me get dressed. No small feat. I now had seven inches of chest to cover with miles of gauze and white tape. That's where angels are helpful. Vicki wrapped endless gauze around me and looked up from her work to say, "Even after surgery, you are still bigger than me."

I could not have had a better send off for a seminar.

I stood facing the audience in new navy suit, gauze

and tape, scars and fears.

I was well into my presentation when all at once I blurted out, as much as a surprise to myself as the stunned audience, "Life is painfully short. I just had cancer. We are here for just a few great moments. Use your time well. It may be all you get."

My voice cracked. It wasn't supposed to. That wasn't part of my well-scripted notes.

The room went deathly silent. It was a silence of sympathy and empathy. For one brief moment one-hundred and fifty of us felt the limits of our days.

Quickly, I was back again on the well-charted course. It wasn't until the end of the hour that I met my second angel.

The audience was on the way out the door. Several gathered around me to shake hands and offer encouragement.

He was tall, about six feet. He strode confidently up to me but forgot to stop. They normally stop. He didn't. He came into my face and kissed me on the lips.

Now, even my friends forget to kiss me good-bye when we part. And here was this stranger, right inside my comfort zone.

"I had cancer, too," he said. "We are part of a select club. A club of survivors. You'll make it, Carol. I feel it."

And with that the prophet left the room and I haven't seen him since. I'd like to meet up with him one day and show him that his prediction was right.

Perhaps he hasn't appeared because I haven't needed him. Maybe he already knows I'm healthy. The angels are out there. I've met two. Sometimes seeing them through the chalkboard dust is difficult. But I know they are in classrooms just like yours.

I have made it, and you will, too. You will, too. We are survivors.

The Lady or the Tiger?

There is a wonderful short story by Frank Richard Stockton called *The Lady or the Tiger?* The plot is simple. A young, poor man falls in love with the king's daughter. She feels the same for him. When the king discovers the lovers, he puts the young man through a barbaric test.

The man must stand in front of two doorways and make a choice. Behind one stands the lovely young maiden. Behind the other stands a hungry tiger. The story ends with the question, "And which will it be, the lady or the tiger?"

The teacher with a longing to leave the classroom has many more options than the young man. In a lifetime, every person has the capabilities to be successful in five careers.

The conscious choice is clearly yours to make.

Make your choice now

You don't have to leave teaching. You don't have to stay in teaching. Not making a decision is still making a decision.

Doing what's right for you will be reward enough.

When do you graduate?

You graduate when you go from marking time to creating a path where you can grow. You graduate when you dare to follow your heart, when you create the bliss you deserve to have.

Your age doesn't limit your potential. You limit your potential. Give up the role of omnipotent ruler. Stop playing God and start playing your best Oscar-winning part— yourself.

Don't wake up at retirement to realize you parked your ladder in the wrong career. What matters most is not how you will feel in ten, fifteen or twenty years. What matters most is how you feel about yourself now.

Discovering I had cancer made me focus on the present. When I stopped living as if I were immortal, I grew up.

Facing my own death helped me face my own life. I learned that the word "no" was a complete sentence. I learned to say yes to the rest of my life.

The teacher longing to leave the classroom needs to leave.

The teacher deciding to stay needs to celebrate. Open the champagne, bring up the band, let's dance.

Let's dance for our survival and our sanity. But most of all let's dance . . . after all this is the celebration of our lives.

I am still teaching . . . are you?

Appendix

August, 19—

Dear _____:

My name is Mrs. Carol Fuery, and I teach your young adult Senior English. I've been a teacher at Cypress Lake High School for the last ten years. I feel lucky to be part of the Cypress Lake family, one of the best schools in Lee County. I especially feel fortunate to have your soon-to-be adult in my classroom.

We will be studying the literature of Great Britain as well as doing weekly writing enhancement papers. I love teaching English Lit. and know that your young adult will be successful in this classroom.

I am a Florida native and received my B.A. degree in English from Florida Atlantic University in Boca Raton. I completed my master's degree in Administration and Supervision from Nova University.

I want to work closely with you. If you have any questions about your young adult's progress please call me at school, 481-2233 or at home, 472-3459.

At school, the best times to reach me are very early in the mornings and between 2:15 and 3:15.

Enclosed you will find a copy of my class rules. I do reward students' efforts frequently with verbal praise, the class honor roll, written praise and congratulatory letters home.

I look forward to working with you this year.

Sincerely,
Carol Fuery

Carol Fuery, English Department
Cypress Lake High School
Panther Lane
Fort Myers, Florida 33907

Dear Parent or Guardian,

October 1, 19—

This is a friendly note to inform you that your "young person," _____ has all writing assignments and other work in. I'm proud of him/her because it takes self-discipline and caring to keep up in my class. So many times we send notes home when there are deficiencies, and not when there is something to praise.

There is a saying, "Catch them doing something good," that is circulating among our schools. I look for the good, and I've found it in _____. With encouragement this pattern will continue.

Sincerely,

Carol Fuery

— — — — — — — — — — — — — — — —

Tear off and send bottom portion to Mrs. Fuery

If you like receiving this message, please write me a brief note on this portion. If you did something special for your "young person" because of their efforts, I'd enjoy knowing about it. Thank you for a minute of your time.

Student's name:

Note:

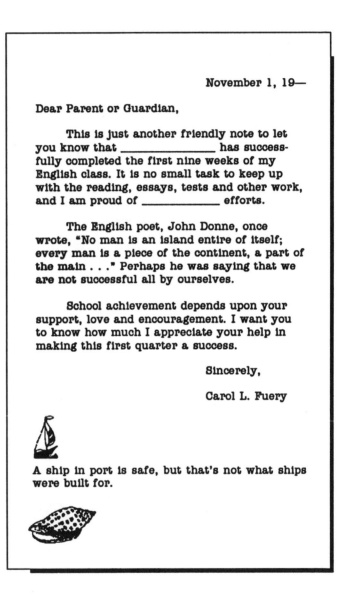

November 1, 19—

Dear Parent or Guardian,

This is just another friendly note to let you know that _____ has successfully completed the first nine weeks of my English class. It is no small task to keep up with the reading, essays, tests and other work, and I am proud of _____ efforts.

The English poet, John Donne, once wrote, "No man is an island entire of itself; every man is a piece of the continent, a part of the main . . ." Perhaps he was saying that we are not successful all by ourselves.

School achievement depends upon your support, love and encouragement. I want you to know how much I appreciate your help in making this first quarter a success.

Sincerely,

Carol L. Fuery

A ship in port is safe, but that's not what ships were built for.

November 1, 19—

Dear Parent or Guardian,

_____ is intelligent, and cares about doing well at school. I feel that the grade he/she earned in this class does not represent the success which is there.

I want all my students to feel good about their progress at school. I have scheduled a conversation with _____ and hope you, also, will talk together.

The future is in _____ hands. I wish a most successful, new nine weeks.

With best regards,

Carol L. Fuery

A ship in port is safe, but that's not what ships were built for.

END OF THE YEAR LETTER

May 22, 19—

Dear Graduate,

I have thoroughly enjoyed teaching you this year. I really appreciate the class of _____.

Your attitude, intelligence and sincerity have made this a wonderful year.

The next years will be turbulent, adventuresome and sometimes insane. Learn from your failures as well as your successes. And with all the changes, try to have a plan.

Remember, a ship in port is safe, but that's not what ships were built for. Try a new tack, take a new direction, one that may be less followed by your friends.

Be brave. You have nothing to lose. You're a child of the universe. You have a right to be here. Make your place in this world that is now before you.

Dreams do come true. Work to make your dreams reality. Good luck. And may God shine His face upon you, and guide your footsteps.

Much love,

Carol L. Fuery

Sample Postcard

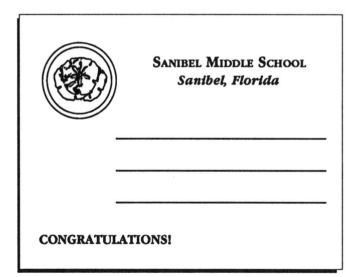

SANIBEL MIDDLE SCHOOL

Dear Parent

It's a pleasure to let you know _____
_____
_____
_____

I enjoy having _____ in my class.

Sincerely,

SANIBEL MIDDLE SCHOOL
Sanibel, Florida

_____

_____

_____

CONGRATULATIONS!

TIME OUT CONDUCT REPORT

Name:

Date:

I was asked to leave Mrs. Fuery's classroom and fill out this sheet. Here is my account of the events that led to my leaving the room.

Did I stop the teaching in this classroom? Explain.

Were other students distracted by what I did?

Put a circle around one of the statements that best fits your mood at the time of the incident:

　　Did I want to get even with someone?
　　Did I want to get revenge?
　　Did I want to feel superior to someone?
　　Did I want to hurt someone?

If you can't answer any of the above questions with a "Yes" then write your own statement that best shows your mood.

I wanted to

_____

Put a check in front of the following statements if they fit your situation. Fill in the appropriate blanks.

　　Did someone get hurt?
　　Was something broken or damaged?
　　Was someone embarrassed?
　　Did I waste my time?
　　Did I waste the teacher's time? How?
　　What did I lose?
　　What did I gain?

What positive things could the teacher do to help us get along better?

What positive things could I do to help myself?

_____
_____

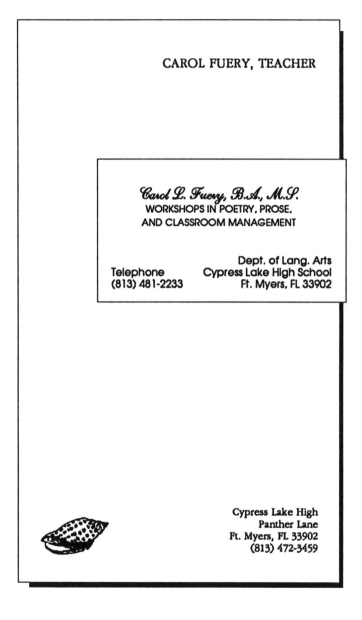

CAROL FUERY, TEACHER

Carol L. Fuery, B.A., M.S.
**WORKSHOPS IN POETRY, PROSE,
AND CLASSROOM MANAGEMENT**

Telephone
(813) 481-2233

**Dept. of Lang. Arts
Cypress Lake High School
Ft. Myers, FL 33902**

Cypress Lake High
Panther Lane
Ft. Myers, FL 33902
(813) 472-3459

Chapter Notes:
A Summary

Christa McAuliffe taught because she wanted to touch the future. And she got her wish. Why do you teach?

Knowing what we want from life is crucial for our happiness.

Our time on earth is finite. Remember that the word "no" is a complete sentence. We can say it sweetly. No.

Taking work home and carrying home problems to work is an inappropriate mix. It destroys balance and harmony. I can't carry papers home every night and have harmony at home.

Does our motivation need a jump start? Make sure the batteries are rechargeable. We recharge our batteries with positive self talk. And if we don't take care of ourselves, who else will?

Letters home let kids and parents know they are doing a good job. Most of us need all the encouragement we can get.

We think in metaphors. Create dreams with pictures attached. If we can imagine it, we can attain it.

Magic cards are magical because they set up an atmosphere of mutual respect and trust. Kids know you care. Only brave teachers with high self-esteem will try magic cards.

In order to win the war, we do not need to eliminate all resistance. Let kids know what they are doing and how they are doing. Feedback is the health food of champions.

The only behavior we can control is our own. Establishing incentives and setting consequences helps us manage kids. Let parents know how their youngsters are doing. Show kids you care by calling home.

The student is our most valued customer. When we began teaching we went into sales. We also entered the entertainment business. Kids buy into our world of praise and encouragement.

The "I know everything" syndrome can become a terminal disease. If you wish to grow, double your risks. Strip away the mask of superiority and be sincere.

We are public relations experts. Teacher begins with a capital T. What you concentrate on, expands. Help your happiness grow by giving it your attention.

Share your expertise. Giving seminars can do wonders for your morale. Keep in mind that there is no guard rail, but the rewards are well worth your best effort.

Our clothes should serve us and help to create our professional image. Remember society expects more from us than any other profession. Look the part.

Foster change. Laugh often. Guard your spiritual health. Listen for the encouragement however muffled and soft it sounds.

Cooperative teaching is just one of many ways to relate to kids. Everyone gets a chance to sit in the big chair.

Sometimes the mid-life crisis feels like a hurricane. Too many relationships run on automatic pilot. Make a change. Set aside daily time together. Share your true feelings. Make the moments count. Listen to the universe's bell schedule.

When you feel the time is right, exit teaching. You have been given the permission to choose. Make your decision now. Do what is right for you. If you decide to stay, play to win, prize fighter.

YOUR TIME

Your sense of time can have a great deal to do with how you feel about your work.

Answer the following questions:

1. Do you have enough time to do the job you're expected to accomplish?
2. Does your teaching leave you enough time to enjoy the other parts of your life?
3. Are you always running into a crisis at school?
4. Are these crises of your own making (you didn't allow enough time to get a job done) or dictated by circumstances outside your control?
5. Do you accomplish more or less when you are free to set your own schedule? Are you better organized in the summer or when school is in session?
6. What would you rather do: take papers home? go in early to complete your work? stay late on certain days to complete work?
7. When you bring school work home, does the work get done? Why or why not?

Did any of these questions touch on a raw spot? That may indicate something you need to think about changing either in your attitude or in your personal time management.

List three things that you could do to improve the way that you are now managing your time.

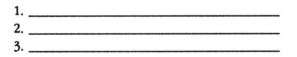

1. _____
2. _____
3. _____

Four fantastic seminars to jump start sagging spirits

1. *Motivating the Ungrateful Dead:*
A Guide to Brain Cell Revival

Equally ideal for kicking off the school year or busting up the mid-term blues, this session focuses on helping teachers learn to build team spirit and foster a sense of caring among their students. In the process, they can't help but muster up their own momentum. Topics include: Our Best Defense Against Boredom, The Five-Step Resistance Plan and Why Report Cards and Paychecks Don't Motivate.

2. *If It's Only Tuesday,*
Why Am I So Frazzled?

In this workshop, Carol details ways to develop timesaving classroom management skills, from "learning to hide" to embracing the computer and the school secretary as two of a teacher's best friends. She outlines ways to overcome procrastination and develop delegation tactics that build personal initiative. The ultimate result is that the teacher accomplishes more, does it faster—and doesn't take home a trunkload of papers every afternoon.

3. *Are You Still Teaching?*
A Survival Session to Keep You Sane

This session is based on the premise that only teachers who are self-assured and motivated can nurture the same attributes in their students. Through classic (and sometimes comical) examples every experienced educator will recognize, Carol describes ways bedraggled veterans can take charge and change the one arena they do control: the classroom.

4. Turning Around the Bad, the Bored and the Belligerent

Filled with sure-fire strategies for winning the games kids play, this session provides a positive, structured approach to managing disruptive behavior. Carol's unmistakable and uplifting message is that teachers CAN create a classroom climate in which most students WANT to behave.

HOW OTHER EDUCATORS GRADE CAROL FUERY ON HER SEMINARS:

"I went back to the classroom with renewed respect for myself and my fellow teachers. My students definitely picked up on my new attitude."
—12-year reacher, Superior, Arizona

"By every standard you are one of the best presenters I have ever heard. You gave many practical ideas that our teachers could implement in their classes immediately. You are truly a teacher of teachers of whom we can all be proud."
—Staff development coordinator, Valdosta, Georgia

"I am sure all our teachers who attended will long remember your 'toxic people' terminology and will be better prepared to react to the 'toxic dump areas' of our schools."
—Staff development director, Raleigh, North Carolina

"I especially liked the way you were able to get right to the heart of teaching, helping us to remove the petty obstacles that so often prevent good teaching."
—Curriculum coordinator, Miami, Florida

Straight from the front line

With more than 20 years in the education profession, Carol Bailey Fuery speaks and writes from experience on subjects ranging from a teacher's first-year fears and frustrations to veteran apathy and exhaustion. The president of Sanddollar Publications, Inc., she's written three books and has won the affection and acclaim of seminar audiences throughout the United States.

Carol has written numerous magazine articles as well as two books of poetry. Her survival series for teachers includes the popular *Winning Year One* for first-year teachers, *Successful Subbing* for substitutes and *Are You Still Teaching?* for experienced educators. She is currently working on another book.

Carol's humor, enthusiasm and straight-forward style have motivated thousands of teachers, principals, superintendents and staff development directors from school districts in major cities and in rural townships.

Whether they participate in her energizing seminars or read her books, her colleagues in education unanimously agree that Carol is "a teacher *of* teachers" who makes them all proud.

***To find out more about
Carol Fuery's books and seminars,
call toll-free***
1-800-330-3459

Three terrific books
to inspire the overwhelmed

1. *Winning Year One: A Survival Manual for First Year Teachers*

With six printings since 1986, *Winning Year One* is Carol Fuery's most popular survival guide. This practical and humorous little manual bridges the gap between college theory (in which no one mentions how to handle irate parents or save face when confronting a talkative, stubborn student in front of his peers) and real-life, classroom experience.

No first-year teacher should be without this inspirational handbook in his or her briefcase.

2. *Successful Subbing: A Survival Guide to Help You Teach Like a Pro*

When teachers are absent, kids can't afford to miss school too. This helpful book tells substitute teachers why trips to the office just don't work, and how to improvise when there's no lesson plan. Other pertinent topics include the often overlooked importance of proper attire, and a daily checklist to make subbing a pleasure instead of a problem.

A must-read for substitutes, this book can also enlighten new teachers.

3. *Are You Still Teaching? A Survival Guide to Keep You Sane*

Carol Fuery's newest book is written for experienced educators who, after years of seemingly thankless work, find themselves feeling overburdened, underpaid and even insecure in their choice of careers. In sometimes tough terms, Carol reminds them that the choice is theirs: Learn to enjoy teaching or get out and do something else. Her expert advice and encouragement could very well be the tonic many teachers with tenure need to help them renew their passion for the profession.

Ordering books is as easy as . . .

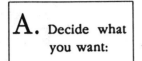

| A. Decide what you want: | *Winning Year One*—$9.95
Successful Subbing — $7.95
Are You Still Teaching?— $13.95 |

Get the set — 3 titles for $29.95
(includes shipping/handling)

Orders under $50 — shipping/handling $3.50

Orders over $50 — *shipping/handling FREE*

Order 10 copies of any title — **SAVE 10%**

B. Have your purchase order number ready.

C. **Then call Sanddollar Publications
toll free number,
1 (800) 330-3459.**

**Or fax your purchase order to
(813) 472-0699.**

No credit cards. Personal checks gladly accepted.

Make payable to: **SSP Inc.,
P.O. Box 461,
Captiva, FL 33924**

*Sanddollar Publications' unconditional guarantee: If
for any reason you are not satisfied with your books,
simply return them for a no-questions-asked, full refund.
Any time. Any reason. No hassles.*